Objects of Adornment

An Exhibition Organized by the Walters Art Gallery and the American Federation of Arts

Objects of Adornment

Five Thousand Years of Jewelry from the Walters Art Gallery, Baltimore

The American Federation of Arts is a national non-profit, educational organization, founded in 1909 to broaden the knowledge and appreciation of the arts of the past and present. Its primary activities are the organization of exhibitions and film programs which travel throughout the United States and abroad, and the fostering of a better understanding among nations by the international exchange of art.

Funding for this project was provided by the Mabel Pew Myrin Trust and the National Endowment for the Arts.

Published by the American Federation of Arts,
41 East 65th Street, New York, New York 10021

LCC 84-72038   ISBN 0-917481-76-X

AFA Exhibition 82-3 / Circulated: October 1984 – February 1987

Many of these essays and photographs originally appeared in *Jewelry: Ancient to Modern,* A Studio Book, Copyright © 1979 by the trustees of the Walters Art Gallery, and are reprinted by permission of Viking Penguin Inc. The photographs were taken by Harry J. Connolly, Jr.

Design & Typography by Howard I. Gralla
Edited by Michaelyn Mitchell
Composed in Syntax types by Finn Typographic Service
Printed by The William J. Mack Company
Bound by Mueller Trade Bindery

Cover: Iris Corsage Ornament. American (New York), ca. 1900. Cat. no. 206

Contents

Acknowledgments

Since its founding in 1909, one of the ongoing commitments of the American Federation of Arts has been the organization of exhibitions of exceptional quality and diversity drawn from important museum collections in this country and abroad. The collaborative efforts involved in organizing such projects provide the unique opportunity to share the vast artistic resources of public collections with other institutions across the country. The Walters Art Gallery is considered to be among one of the most important comprehensive art museums in America, and as Robert Bergman discusses in his introduction, until recently the wealth of its collections has been virtually unknown to the general public. It is most appropriate that in 1984—a year in which the AFA is celebrating its seventy-fifth anniversary and the Walters is commemorating its fiftieth year as a public museum—the two institutions have joined together to organize and tour *Objects of Adornment: Five Thousand Years of Jewelry from the Walters Art Gallery, Baltimore.*

Many people have helped make this project possible. Thanks are due the trustees of the Walters Art Gallery for their generosity in making the material available for a national tour; Robert P. Bergman, Director of the Walters, for his continued support of the project; William Johnston, Assistant Director and Chief Curator, for initially proposing the exhibition to the AFA and assisting on all aspects of the project; and the Walters' curatorial staff and former Director, Richard H.

Randall, Jr., for selecting the objects and contributing to the publication.

We would also like to acknowledge the important contributions of the following individuals at the Walters: Terry Weisser, Director of Conservation and Technical Research, Carol Snow, Assistant Objects Conservator, Helen Ingalls, Conservation Intern, Donna Strahan, Contract Conservator, and Katie Franetovich, Free-lance Technical Assistant, for their careful and professional preparation of the objects for the tour; Susan Tobin, Theresa Brown, and Ruth Silk of the Photography Department for new photography and the collection and coordination of photographic material for the project; Harry J. Connolly, Jr., the Walters' former staff photographer; and Leopoldine Arz, Registrar, and Betsy Binckley, Assistant Registrar, for their patient and thorough review of cataloguing data and other registrarial and administrative responsibilities related to the tour.

Members of the AFA staff also deserve mention for their important contributions: Jane S. Tai, Associate Director and Exhibition Program Director, for her initial planning and supervision of the project; Jeffery J. Pavelka, Assistant Director, Exhibition Program, for guiding the development of both the exhibition and publication and carrying the project to completion; Amy McEwen, Coordinator, Scheduling, for diligently working out the itinerary for the exhibition; Carol O'Biso, Registrar, and Susan MacGill, Assistant Registrar, for their conscientious coordination with the conservators and registrars at the Walters and their careful handling and supervision of the objects in the exhibition; Sandra Gilbert, Public Information Director, and Lindsay South, Public Information Coordinator, for arranging the publicity for the national tour with the Walters; and Fran Falkin, Konrad G. Kuchel, Mary Ann Monet, and Teri Roiger for their varied skills and support. Our appreciation also extends to Michaelyn Mitchell, Assistant to the Director, for her thorough editing of the catalogue.

We also wish to express our appreciation to Howard I. Gralla for designing the catalogue, the poster, and the exhibition graphics; to Robin Parkinson for designing the installation cases; and to Dorothy Globus for her assistance in planning the layout of the exhibition.

Finally, we are deeply grateful to the Mabel Pew Myrin Trust and the National Endowment for the Arts for their generous financial support of this project.

Wilder Green
Director
The American Federation of Arts

Introduction

In 1984-85 the Walters Art Gallery is celebrating its Golden Jubilee Year, the fiftieth anniversary of its opening in 1934 as a public museum. We are proud to commemorate this milestone by joining with the American Federation of Arts in presenting *Objects of Adornment,* an exhibition drawn from the Walters' renowned collection of historical jewelry. The Walters Art Gallery has long been considered by scholars and cognoscenti among the most important comprehensive art museums in the United States, but until recently the public has remained relatively unaware of the range and importance of the Gallery's collections—and with good reason: until the dedication of its new wing in 1974, eighty percent of the Walters' holdings remained in storage. Happily, however, since 1974 the situation has been reversed. Our Golden Jubilee coincides, then, with the tenth anniversary of the collection's first comprehensive presentation to the public. *Objects of Adornment* only hints at the variety and quality of the Gallery's collections.

William Thompson Walters (1819-1894) was a young engineer from Pennsylvania who moved to Baltimore in 1841. There he staked his future on his adopted city's strategic commercial location, and his choice was most propitious. Following a string of business successes, Walters became a founder and principal stockholder of the Atlantic Coast Line Railroad, which was to be the basis of his fortune.

William liked to say that the first dollar he earned had been spent on a work of art. His first acquisitions were of American art, but by the time of the Civil War, during most of which he was in Paris, he had turned his attention to the three areas on which his acquisitions would remain focused for the remainder of his life: contemporary European (especially French) painting, oriental ceramics, and the sculpture of Antoine-Louis Barye. With George A. Lucas as his mentor, Walters visited the salons and ateliers of Paris, purchasing and even commissioning works from such luminaries as Corot, Daumier, and Gérôme. His interest in oriental ceramics was inspired by a visit in 1862 to London's Crystal Palace, where he saw the exhibition of Sir Rutherford Alcock's collection. Eventually he was to amass a collection of approximately fifteen hundred pieces of Far Eastern and Islamic ceramics. Walters' attraction to Barye's sculpture has provided Baltimore with one of this country's pre-eminent collections of that artist's work, including several large-scale bronzes that serve as the chief ornaments of Baltimore's historic Mt. Vernon Place. After Barye's death William Walters served as president of the committee founded to erect a monument to the artist in Paris.

In the late 1870s Earl Shinn wrote a far-ranging survey of art in America entitled *The Art Treasures of America,* in which he described William Walters' gallery—which was opened to the public at specified times during the year (the entry fee being donated to the poor)—as "an educator of taste not to be excelled in the New World." Happily (and unlike the collections of almost all of his contemporaries), William Walters' collection remains intact—at the Walters Art Gallery.

From his father, Henry Walters (1848-1931) inherited the twin mantles of railroad magnate and art collector, and in both areas he enlarged William's already-substantial achievements. His business success was enormous—he expanded the railroad and associated ventures such as the Safe-Deposit and Trust Company of Baltimore (now the Mercantile Safe-Deposit and Trust Company)—and was more than equalled by the prodigious and perspicacious nature of his art collecting. Between 1893 and 1931, with particular intensity during the 1920s, Henry assembled one of the most distinguished and surely the most wide-ranging of all American private art collections. Whereas William had restricted his acquisitions to several strictly defined areas, Henry's were characterized by a rare catholicity of taste. Beginning with his purchase in 1893 of a group of ancient Near Eastern seals from the dealer Dikran Kelekian, almost nothing escaped Henry Walters' vision. Renaissance painting; medieval enamels, ivories, and goldsmiths' work; illuminated manuscripts; Islamic metalwork; Greek and Roman sculpture; Egyptian antiquities; Sèvres porcelain; Renaissance bronzes; Byzantine art; arms and armor; Chinese sculpture; jewelry of all periods—these were only a few of his interests.

Among Henry's favored dealers were Kelekian and the Seligman brothers; Joseph Brummer, Bernhard Berenson, and others also provided advice and access to works of art. Most of the material in the collection, however, was selected and acquired piece by piece by Henry himself, much of it during his worldwide travels. His yacht, the *Narada,* must have been like a floating museum on its return crossings to the United States after stops in ports as distant as Constantinople and St. Petersburg. In 1900, while the *Narada* was moored alongside the Czar's yacht in St. Petersburg Harbor, Henry was visiting the shop of Peter Carl Fabergé. That day's purchases are still at the Gallery.

Henry Walters made several outstanding purchases of collections en bloc. The most important of these was the acquisition in 1902 from Don Marcello Massarenti of the entire contents of the family palace in Rome, the Palazzo Accoramboni. Included were more than fifteen hundred works of art, among them seven monumental marble sarcophagi excavated near the Via Salaria that today form the most imposing ensemble of Roman relief sculpture in the United States. Most of the Walters' Italian Renaissance paintings also come from the Massarenti Collection.

Prior to this gargantuan acquisition, Walters' collection was kept in the family's Mt. Vernon Place townhouse and the annexes to it that William had built, but with the purchase of the Massarenti Collection, considerably more space was needed. Thus between 1904 and 1908 the Renaissance revival building that was to be the original Walters Art Gallery was constructed. Today this landmark structure houses the Walters' collection of Renaissance painting, sculpture, and smaller-scale arts.

Henry lived most of his adult life in New York; but he sent all but his most favored purchases to his private gallery in Baltimore, and the crates of art shipped there during the teens and twenties were legendary. Many of them, however, remained tightly shut. Neither the collection nor the man were without an air of mystery about them.

Henry served as a member of the Board of Trustees of the Metropolitan Museum of Art, and it was assumed that his collection was destined to become part of that great museum. Indeed, Henry had enriched the Metropolitan with several important gifts of art over the years. What a surprise it must have been to all concerned to learn at the time of Walters' death in 1931 that he had bequeathed the entire collection—some twenty-five thousand works of art—along with the Walters Art Gallery building, Walters House, and an endowment to the city of Baltimore, his birthplace, "for the benefit of the people."

Following Walters' death, a now-legendary band of young curators was recruited—Dorothy Miner, Dorothy Kent Hill, Marvin C. Ross, George Heard Hamilton, and Edward F. King—and three years later, on November 3, 1934, the Walters Art Gallery opened its doors to the public. The rest, as they say, is history. Today, the Walters Art Gallery stands as one of Baltimore's premier civic institutions.

The jewelry selected for this exhibition represents the chronological range of Henry Walters' collecting: the earliest works date from about 3000 B.C., and the latest were created during the first years of the twentieth century. The highlights are too numerous to isolate in this brief introduction, but one cannot help but mention the Olbia Treasure in the ancient material, the great Visigothic eagle brooches and the Byzantine jewelry in the medieval selection, the Renaissance pendant collection, and among the modern pieces the tours-de-force created by Lalique and Tiffany & Co. When the jewelry collection was first exhibited as a whole at the Walters in 1979, it caused nothing less than a sensation.

The vast majority of the jewelry presented here was collected by Henry Walters during the first three decades of this century, but a number of important pieces have been added to the collection in the ensuing years—some, purchases on the part of discerning curators and others, gifts on the part of discriminating and generous donors.

The work of the Gallery's curators (several of whom are among the authors of this publication), conser-

vators, registrars, preparators, photographers, and publications specialists has made this complex exhibition possible. To them, to our colleagues at the American Federation of Arts who have organized the traveling exhibition, and to those who have provided the necessary financial support for the whole enterprise, the Walters extends its congratulations and its gratitude.

William and Henry Walters always intended the public to share the joys and benefits of their art collection. The Walters Art Gallery in Baltimore is the permanent instrument of their philanthropic and cultural commitment, and *Objects of Adornment* is an extension of that same spirit.

Robert P. Bergman
Director
The Walters Art Gallery

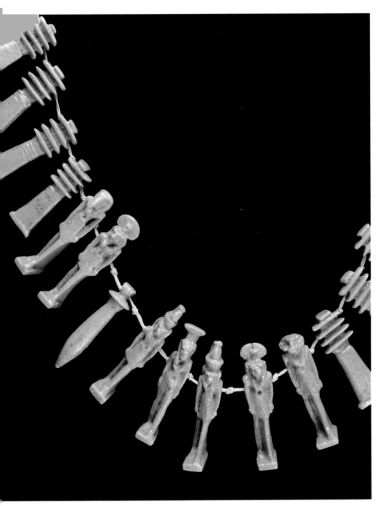

I. Cat. no. 11

II. Cat. no. 17

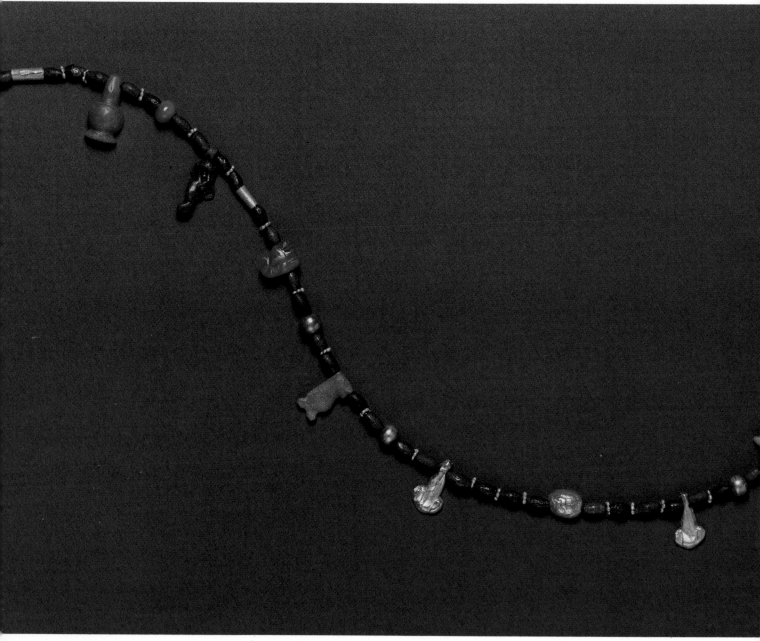

III. Cat. no. 9

IV. Cat. no. 25

V. Cat. no. 30

VI. Cat. no. 43

VII. Cat. no. 49

VIII. Cat. no. 53

IX. Cat. no. 63

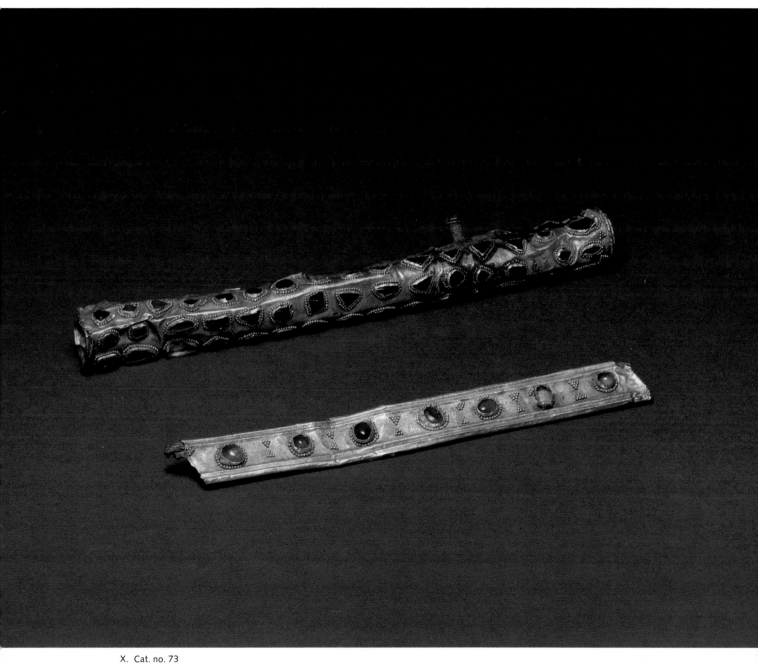

X. Cat. no. 73

XII. Cat. no. 112

XIII. Cat. no. 114

XI. Cat. no. 89

XIV. Cat. no. 137

XV. Cat. no. 139

XVI. Cat. no. 157

XVII. Cat. no. 157

XVIII. Cat. no. 186

XIX. Cat. no. 207

XX. Cat. no. 209

XXII. Cat. no. 212

XXI. Cat. no. 210

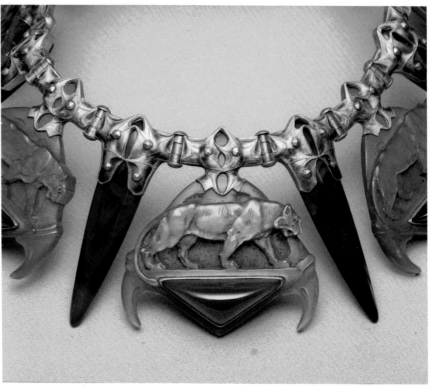

XXIII. Cat. no. 213

Ancient Near Eastern Jewelry

The civilizations that flourished in Asia from Iran westwards to the Mediterranean between 3000 B.C. and the conquest of Alexander the Great in the fourth century B.C. are usually grouped together as the ancient Near East, a general term covering such diverse peoples as the Sumerians, whose language was unrelated to any other, the Semitic-speaking Babylonians and Assyrians, and the Indo-European Persians of Iran in the east; and in the west the Semitic Canaanites and Hebrews and the Indo-European Hittites of Asia Minor, to name only the most familiar. The political situation in the area shifted endlessly, often violently; nevertheless, we may legitimately think of the ancient Near East as a cultural entity, for the civilizations there shared many traditions. This was in part due to far-ranging trade, which developed very early because of the area's uneven distribution of natural resources. A major impetus for trade was the demand for the brightly colored stones and gleaming metals with which to make jewelry. One might even claim this demand as a civilizing agent in the ancient Near East. It is at least of historical significance that the ''cradle of civilization,'' ancient Sumer in southern Iraq, where writing and the concept of cities were invented, had neither stone nor metal. The Sumerians' quest for gold and silver from as far as the west coast of Turkey and for lapis lazuli from Afghanistan must have been instrumental in spreading knowledge of their civilized ways throughout the area.

It is appropriate that the first items in this catalogue of magnificent jewelry should be simple stone amulets from the heartland of the ancient Near East. These well-worn talismans, painstakingly repaired in antiquity, are a reminder of the original purpose of jewelry as something magical worn on the body to protect the wearer or increase his powers. In the ancient world jewelry never quite lost this amuletic significance. This is obvious in ancient Egypt, where symbols, like the signs in the hieroglyphic script, remained in the form of representational pictures. It is less apparent in the ancient Near East, for there writing and symbols took on abstract forms in very early times. We know, however, that rosettes, stars, floral elements, and quadruple spirals had religious significance. Jewelry was given as a votive to the gods and was also worn by those statues of the gods used in ritual. It also constituted a significant part of the treasuries of the temples, which were important economic units of the ancient cities.

Evidence for the history of jewelry in the ancient Near East is at once rich, sporadic, and contradictory. That actual examples of this jewelry are rare is not surprising in light of the turbulent history of the area and the frequent sacking of cities and, presumably, of royal tombs and graveyards as well. Only a few undisturbed burials, such as the Royal Tombs of Ur in Sumer or Alaca Hüyük in Asia Minor, have been discovered. None of the burials of the great rulers of empire, which may have vied in richness with those in Egypt, have been found intact. Of the great treasuries stored in palaces and temples, we have only a few hoards, hastily gathered and hidden in time of siege. Such treasuries are likely to be a hodgepodge of primitive and fine work, local and imported pieces, contemporary jewels and some thousands of years old—mixtures that reflect the other important function of jewelry in ancient times: in a world without coinage, it served as a measure of wealth and a means of exchange. Because of its intrinsic value, jewelry was accumulated from many sources and kept for generations. In trying to isolate the various sources of pieces in a treasure, we are helped by a few hoards from jewelers' workshops and a greater number of ancient jewelry molds.

Ancient Near Eastern texts tell us how much jewelry we are missing. Jewelry is included in inventories of temple treasuries and royal dowries, lists of tribute and booty, and descriptions of gifts. The representation of jewelry in art, on the other hand, is sometimes misleading. The greatest collection of ancient Near Eastern jewelry comes from the Royal Tombs at Ur in ancient Sumer, which date to the second half of the third millennium B.C. In this series of burials, some of them sacrificial, the dead were richly, even gaudily, bedecked with headdresses, necklaces, earrings, rings, hair ornaments, and pins of gold, silver, lapis lazuli, and carnelian. The techniques of polishing and cutting hard stone, solid casting, repoussé, granulation, and filigree work in gold were already highly developed. Thick gold chains, with loops interlocked to form a square section, could be made. On the statues representing the upper classes of the period, however, no jewelry at all is shown. In fact, until the ninth century B.C. only very simple jewelry is seen on statues of royalty or officials—on those of women, a high collar necklace; on those of men, a single strand of heavy beads; and on either, an occasional simple bracelet. Amulets strung around the neck are seen in some Syrian frescoes from about 1800 B.C. Only on crude clay figurines or plaques representing votaries (often nude women) or deities can the elaborate jewelry of the Ur tombs be matched. It is not yet clear what this contradictory evidence as to fashions in jewelry means. The statues surviving from these times represent people in pious attitudes, and it may be that there was some restriction against wearing finery "in church." The palace reliefs that began to be made in the ninth century B.C. in Assyria and Syria are more secular in nature, and this may be why people are shown wearing a great deal of jewelry: diadems, earrings, necklaces, bracelets, armlets, as well as crowns and robes studded with gold appliqués. Syrian ivories of the period show women in elaborate headdresses. Actual examples of jewelry from this period are, however, extremely rare.

The jewelry seen on figures in the Assyrian reliefs obviously comes from several sources. Some pieces may have been tribute or booty. Foreign types may also have been made in Assyria, since craftsmen from all over the ancient Near East were brought to work at court. In sorting out the different types represented on the reliefs, stylistic analysis based on other forms of art is not very helpful, for jewelry is seldom representational. Burials of simple folk are, on the other hand, invaluable guides in isolating regional traditions. We know, for instance, that bracelets with stylized lions' heads (Cat. no. 7), which are so often seen on Assyrian reliefs, were actually native to the mountains of Iran. It is probable that our knowledge of ancient Near Eastern jewelry will always depend on finds in such areas—places that were in contact with the great centers of civilization but off the beaten track of sacking armies. In fact, it is only by assembling many different kinds of evidence for jewelry that a picture can be drawn from the sketchy remains of this rich but turbulent past.

Jeanny Vorys Canby

Notes: The very nature of the material has long prevented a comprehensive survey of ancient Near Eastern jewelry, but K. R. Maxwell-Hyslop's pioneering work *Western Asiatic Jewelry, c. 3000-612 B.C.* (Methuen's Handbook of Archaeology, London, 1971) has done much to improve the situation.

1

Pendant

Mesopotamian, ca. 3000 B.C.
Height: ¹¹/₁₆ in. (1.8 cm)
Purchased from Sotheby and Company, Sale, London,
November 26, 1968, lot 20. (42.1462)

Smoothly carved of red-brown stone, this frog pendant
is flat on the back side and perforated sideways above
the feet. This simple amulet and the one that follows
(Cat. no. 2) show signs of wear and ancient repairs.
Both are of a type known from the Protoliterate period,
a period in ancient Mesopotamia before writing.

Notes: For specific parallels see Max Mallowan, "Excavations at Braq
and Chagar Bazar," *Iraq*, British School of Archaeology in Iraq 9,
London, 1947, pls. X:3, XIV, 1:17, XV:6, 7, 15.

2

Pendant

Mesopotamian, ca. 3000 B.C.
Length: ⅞ in. (2.2 cm)
Purchased from Sotheby and Company, Sale, London,
November 26, 1968, lot 20. (42.1456)

This pink stone amulet is carved in the shape of a single
claw. It is of a type known from the Protoliterate
period.

Notes: See notes for Catalogue number 1.

3

Armlet

Mesopotamian, early first millennium B.C.
Diameter: 3 ³/₁₆ in. (8.1 cm)
Purchased by Henry Walters from Edgar Banks as
"from Ur," 1930. (57.621)

This heavy solid-silver armlet tapers towards the ends,
which are shaped like nail heads and decorated by
incised lines. The diameter of the piece suggests that it
was worn on the upper arm. The bracelet, which is one
of a pair, was so heavily covered with corrosion that it
was originally classified as bronze. A similar pair of
armlets, made of gold, was excavated in 1922 in the
ancient E-nun-mah Temple at Ur under a floor of the
Persian period (sixth century B.C.); however, this hoard
contained objects from as far back as the late third
millennium B.C. and therefore cannot provide a certain
date for the bracelet shown here.

Notes: For the Ur armlets see Sir C. Leonard Woolley, *The Neo-Baby-
lonian and Persian Periods*, Ur Excavations, vol. 9, The University
Museum of the University of Pennsylvania and The British Museum,
London, 1962, U 457 pl. 21, pp. 29 ff., 106.

Cat. no. 1   Cat. no. 2

Cat. no. 3

Cat. no. 4

4

Ring

Ancient Syrian, second millennium B.C.
Diameter: $^{11}/_{16}$ in. (1.8 cm)
Height: 1⅞ in. (4.8 cm)
Publications: Zahn, *Schiller*, no. 106 c, p. 52, pl. 46;
Robert Zahn, *Illustrated London News*, March 16,
1929, fig. 6; Canby, *Ancient Near East*, no. 24; William
Culican, "The Case for the Baurat Schiller Crowns,"
JWAG, vol. 35, 1977, pp. 30 ff., figs. 9, 10.
Acquired by Henry Walters from the Bachstitz Gallery,
Berlin (?), 1929. (57.970)

This heavy ring with chased details is cast of gold or
electrum. The hoop is elaborately decorated with lotus
blossoms in relief and bands of crudely chased geometric designs. On the bezel lies a well-modeled ram. This
seems to be a provincial version of an elaborate type of
Egyptian ring of the New Kingdom period.

Notes: For Egyptian rings see Aldred, *Jewels*, pl. 91, p. 217.

5

Earring

Ancient Syrian, eleventh-tenth century B.C.
Height: 1 $^{5}/_{16}$ in. (3.3 cm)
Acquired by Henry Walters (?) before 1931. (57.608)

This earring, one of a pair, seems to be a variant of a
type of earring with pendant "mulberry" elements that
has been found in Syria, Palestine, Cyprus, and Iran in a
late-second-millennium B.C. context. From a tall triangular ear wire hangs a cluster of five biconical gold
beads that are attached together at pointed ends. The
bead at the top is flanked by hollow disks; the one at
the bottom has a cluster of four granules. The beads are
made in two halves in repoussé.

Notes: For the closest parallel see K. R. Maxwell-Hyslop, *Western
Asiatic Jewelry c. 3000-612 B.C.*, Methuen's Handbook of Archaeology, London, 1971, pp. 225 ff., pl. 200 (right).

Cat. no. 5

Cat. no. 6

6

Pendant

Ancient Iranian, ca. 1000 B.C. (?)
Height: 1 in. (2.5 cm)
Publications: Canby, *Ancient Near East*, no. 39.
Provenance unknown. (47.96)

This glass pendant in the form of a ram's head has large
holes drilled up under the chin. The face and ears are
white with lines of black and yellow, the eyes are black
surrounded by yellow, and the horns and jaws are

black. Pendants such as this were thought to be Etruscan, but the recent discovery of a similar pendant in Iran, where sophisticated glass working is attested in the early first millennium B.C., suggests that area as the center of manufacture.

Notes: For Etruscan examples see *BMCJ*, no. 1454, pl. XXIII, p. 143 (no. 1453); for the example from Iran, see Oscar W. Muscarella, ''Excavations at Dinkh Tepe 1966,'' *BMMA*, vol. 27, 1968, p. 194, fig. 19.

Cat. no. 7

7
Bracelet

Ancient Iranian, ninth century B.C. (?)
Diameter: 2¼ in. (5.7 cm)
Purchased by Henry Walters from Dikran Kelekian in a group of Luristan bronzes in 1931; said by him to be ''from Nehavend, Persia.'' (54.125)

The terminals of this cast bronze bracelet are in the shape of lions' heads. Recessed triangles over the snout and between the ears presumably held inlays. The underside of each head is hollow. This feature, together with the mint condition of the piece and the

presence of zinc in the metal, casts doubt on the authenticity.

Notes: For bracelets of this type see K. R. Maxwell-Hyslop, *Western Asiatic Jewelry*, Methuen's Handbook of Archaeology, London, 1971, pp. 246 ff., fig. 230; for a discussion of zinc in such bronzes, see P. R. S. Moorey, *Catalogue of the Ancient Persian Bronzes in The Ashmolean Museum*, Oxford, 1971, pp. 298 ff.

8
Fibula Clasp

Urartian, eighth century B.C. (?)
Height: 1⅜ in. (3.5 cm)
Old label ''P 2124''; purchased by Henry Walters from Joseph Brummer, 1925. (54.2232)

This ancient type of brooch is in the form of a griffin with its head turned sideways. The hand on the foreleg would have held the pin. Cast of bronze (?), the piece has sockets reserved for inlaid eyes and brow. The tail is pierced for an attachment. The bird has a spiral crest, below which a stiff ruff runs to the shoulders. Semiovals mark the neck feathers. The muscles of the foreleg are indicated by a tulip pattern; those of the back leg, by curved lines. The fierce head of the beast and other stylistic details recall works from ancient Urartu (modern Armenia).

Notes: For good photographs of bronze furniture elements of the same style from the Haldi Temple at Toprak-kale, see Guitty Azarpay, *Urartian Art and Artefacts: A Chronological Study*, Berkeley, 1968, pls. 51, 54 (head turned sideways).

Cat. no. 8

Ancient Egyptian Jewelry

One of the more appealing aspects of the long-lived civilization that flourished in the Nile valley from before 3000 B.C. down to Roman times was the cheerful belief that life in the next world was much like life in this world. The corresponding notion that the things of this life were needed in the next is responsible for the wealth of well-preserved jewelry from tombs in ancient Egypt that has survived to our own times. Unlike what remains from the ancient Near East, much of this is royal jewelry. The now-familiar treasures of King Tut-ankh-amun are but the richest in a long series of royal jewels going back as far as the first historic dynasty, about 3000 B.C. Jewelry inscribed with the name of the owner, making it easy to date, as well as the wonderful pictures on the walls of tombs showing jewels being worn and ancient jewelers at work, have provided a wealth of evidence from which to study ancient Egyptian jewelry.

Some of the jewelry from tombs, although exquisitely made, is obviously too fragile to have been worn and must have been made specifically for use in the other world; but some of it shows signs of having been worn. If the provenance is not known, however, it is often impossible to distinguish between "personal" and "funerary" jewelry, unless it is specifically connected with the iconography of the afterlife. Nor was this distinction necessarily of great importance to the ancients. Amulets form one of the largest categories of extant Egyptian jewelry, for it was the custom to place these within the wrappings of the mummy. These amulets, however, are nearly always provided with a means of suspension, indicating that they were still conceived of as something that could be worn.

As in the ancient Near East, in Egypt jewelry was worn by men and women, as well as by statues of the gods. Here, too, it served as a measure of wealth and a means of exchange. Heavy gold collars were the standard royal reward for officials and generals. With the great demand for jewelry in this life and the next, it is no wonder that the craft developed at an early date into a complex and refined art. The infinite patience and rigorously high standards characteristic of Egyptian artisans is nowhere more evident than in the jewelry they produced. Working only with bronze and stone tools, open braziers, and blow pipes, they created exquisite pieces that can equal those of the better-equipped jewelers of later times.

Egypt was fortunate in having at hand (from the desert to the east or from Sinai) an abundance of raw materials with which to make jewelry: gold, turquoise, agate, and amethyst. Silver and lapis lazuli, however, had to be imported. Glazes and glass-like substances were also used extensively as substitutes for precious stones. It did not take the Egyptians long to discover that steatite, which is easy to carve, would take a glaze and become hardened in the firing process. Faience, a vitreous paste that self-glazes to a beautiful blue-green when fired, was also discovered early. True glass, with the bright opaque colors the Egyptians preferred, was produced in the New Kingdom (ca. 1500-1100 B.C.), when it was, strangely enough, cut and inlaid in cloisons rather than fused into them as in real enamel work.

Necklaces were particularly popular in Egypt, the most typical form being a wide collar that lay in a broad circle below the throat. Heavy bead necklaces and pectorals were also popular. Diadems, armlets, girdles, bracelets, anklets, and various hair ornaments were also worn, but earrings, which were always popular in the ancient Near East, were not introduced into Egypt until the beginning of the New Kingdom (ca. 1500 B.C.). Most of this jewelry had amuletic significance. The exquisite little pendant figures, of which there are so many, represent deities or their sacred animals and were used as talismans to help or protect the wearer. Elegant amulets have been found strung on twine or clustered on a wire, with no apparent interest in the aesthetics of the arrangement. The elements of the intricate and pleasing designs are usually hieroglyphs with symbolic meaning.

The familiar scarab represents a dung beetle, an insect the Egyptians believed to be self-created from the ball they observed it rolling. Because they associated this behavior with the rising and setting of the sun, the beetle took on the amuletic significance of creation, rebirth, and power. The earliest rings were merely scarabs tied to the finger. Crudely knotted gold wire replaced the string, and eventually a more elegant hoop was devised. The bottom of the scarab was sometimes flattened and decorated. Later it was inscribed with a person's name, and this led to the development , centuries later, of the signet ring.

It is often impossible to date Egyptian pieces, in part because of the amuletic character of the jewelry. Understandably, there was little innovation in the representation of sacred or magical subjects over the years; furthermore, a lively conservatism is the very essence of Egyptian art. Forms developed in the earliest periods remained standard for thousands of years, although they seldom became static or dull. Paradoxically, the very wealth of well-dated court jewelry has contributed to the problem of dating pieces, for it has postponed the tiresome analysis of minute stylistic differences that poorer material demands. The royal jewels of Egypt have understandably dazzled all eyes.

Jeanny Vorys Canby

The inscriptions in this section have been translated by Hans Goedicke, Professor of Near Eastern Studies at Johns Hopkins University. The chronology is based on that in Cyril Aldred's *Jewels of the Pharaohs: Egyptian Jewelry of the Dynastic Period,* Praeger, New York, 1971, and George Steindorff's *Catalogue of the Egyptian Sculpture in The Walters Art Gallery,* Baltimore, 1946.

9

Necklace

Egyptian, New Kingdom (?) (sixteenth-twelfth century B.C.)
Length: 19 5/16 in. (49.1 cm)
Height of cornflowers: 1/2 in. (1.3 cm)
Purchased by Henry Walters from Dikran Kelekian before 1931. (57.1516)

Beads of gold, blue faience, and carnelian are interspersed in a modern arrangement with thin gold beads decorated with granulation and eleven amulets. At either end of the necklace are the familiar cornflower pendants carved of carnelian; next, crude faience pendants (jackals' heads?); then, hippopota-

muses' heads carved of carnelian. Next at left is the hippopotamus goddess, Toeris (patroness of birth), carved from a thin sliver of light blue glass, matched at right with a fly (a military emblem) cast of shiny, light blue glass. Next are hollow gold pendant-amulets in the shape of serpents' heads. These are flat on the back and have sketchy details in repoussé on the top. In the center of the necklace is a gold scarab-shaped bead made in the same way. The New Kingdom date is suggested by the use of glass.

Notes: For jackal-head amulets see Petrie, *Amulets,* no. 22; for hippopotamus-head amulets see ibid., no. 237; for snake-head amulets see ibid., no. 97. All three are *apotropaic* (evil-averting). The fly, ibid., no. 19, is also used as a hieroglyph. See Alan H. Gardiner, *Egyptian Grammar: Being an Introduction to the Study of Hieroglyphs,* Oxford, 1927.

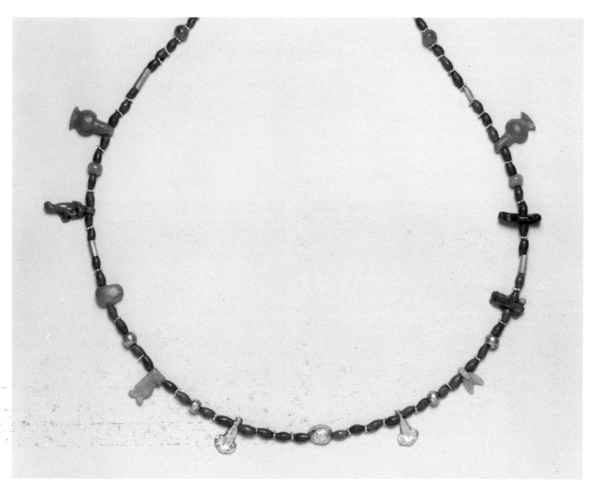

Cat. no. 9 (see colorplate III)

10

Pectoral

Egyptian, n.d.
Height: 3¾ in. (9.5 cm)
Width: 4 in. (10.2 cm)
Purchased by Henry Walters (?), 1929. (42.91)

Large pendants, or pectorals, in the shape of the facade of a shrine, were an important item of Egyptian funerary jewelry. The front side often had an overhanging cornice, and the center, a heart scarab (a substitute for the real heart of the deceased). Sometimes the scarab was inscribed with magical spells. Depicted on these pectorals were the gods of the afterworld: Osiris (or his *djed* pillar), chief god of the dead; his wife, Isis, and her sister, Nephthys (or the *tyet*, the girdle knot symbolizing them); and the ape of the god Thoth or the jackal of the god Anubis, both of whom were involved in the weighing of a person's heart. These pectorals were usually perforated by holes that ran from the top edge of the piece to the back side so that the attachment would not be seen.

On this glazed steatite pectoral traces of red paste remain—red in the background areas and blue beneath

the boat. Triangles are inlaid in the paste between the lotus blossoms on the front side. Standing in a boat are two apes of Thoth with their paws raised as if to support the scarab attached to the central oval recess. On the back is seated Osiris, whose notched garment suggests his role as a grain god. He is adored by a woman in a flowing gown with a perfume cone on her head. Between the figures a *djed* pillar has arms raised to support an oval, which may have held another scarab. All four hieroglyphic inscriptions read *Osiris.* This pectoral is of a well-known, non-royal type.

Notes: See Erike Feucht, *Pektorale nichtköniglicher Personen,* Ägyptologische Abhandlungen 22 (eds. Wolfgang Helck, Eberhard Otto), Wiesbaden, 1971, no. 99 A, pl. XIV, nos. 107 B, E, pl. XVI, no. 108 B, pl. XVII.

11

Amuletic Necklace

Egyptian, n.d.
Length: 15¼ in. (38.7 cm)
Height of *djed* pillars: 1⅛ in. (2.9 cm)
Publications: Steindorff, *Catalogue,* no. 459,

Cat. no. 10

Cat. no. 10

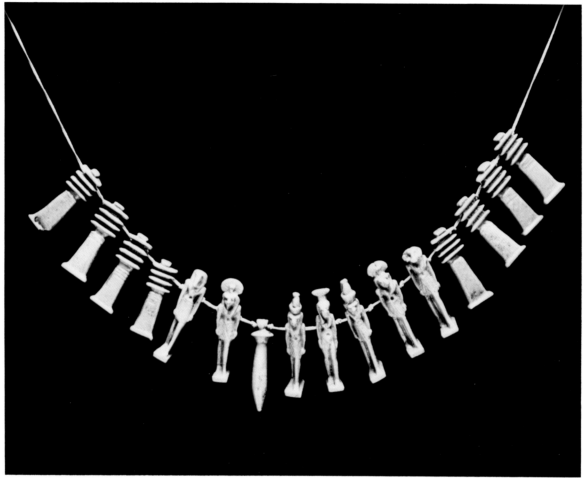

Cat. no. 11 (see colorplate I)

pl. LXXVII, nos. 563, 564, 568, 569, 584, 592, pl. LXXXVIII.
Acquired by Henry Walters (?) before 1931.
(48.1685-99)

Amulets were an important part of funerary equipment, and the position in which some of them were laid on mummies suggests that they were thought of as jewelry. The deities most frequently depicted on these amulets are Isis, wife of Osiris, the great god of the nether world; her son, Horus-the-Child (the Greek Harpocrates), who is shown as a nude youth with a side lock, sucking his thumb; Nephthys, the sister of Isis; the ram-head god, Khnum, creator of mankind; the falcon-headed Horus, wearing a double crown (symbolizing his position as national god) or a disk (symbolizing his role as god of heaven); and the ibis-headed Thoth, god of wisdom (literature and science), or his sacred animals, the ibis or baboon.

At either end of this necklace of light blue faience are four *djed* pillars, symbols of Osiris. Following these at left are Thoth, Horus wearing a disk, a papyrus column, Isis flanked by Horus wearing a double crown, Horus wearing a disk, and Khnum. The amulets have been restrung in the order of those found on a mummy at Hawara. Behind the figures are pillars, which are pierced at shoulder level.

Cat. no. 12

12
Pendant

Egyptian, n.d.
Height: 1 9/16 in. (4.0 cm)
Publications: Steindorff, *Catalogue*, no. 404, pl. LXX.
Acquired by Henry Walters (?) before 1931. (42.346)

This lapis lazuli amulet depicts the goddess Isis seated on a throne decorated with a scale pattern. She holds her left breast and raises the head of infant Horus on her lap. The broad face and squat proportions may

indicate an early date. The back is perforated at shoulder level.

13
Amulet

Egyptian, n.d.
Height: ¾ in. (1.9 cm)
Collection of Carmichael (sale catalogue, *Antiquities of the Collection of the Late Lord Carmichael of Skirling*, Sotheby and Company, London, Wednesday, June 9, 1926, lot no. 235); purchased by Henry Walters from Dikran Kelekian, 1926. (42.195)

The feet of this black-speckled carnelian representation of Horus-the-Child have broken off, but the angle of the legs suggests he was seated on his mother's lap. A loop protruding from the shoulders is also broken off.

14
Pendant Amulet

Egyptian, n.d.
Height: 9/16 in. (1.4 cm)
Publications: Steindorff, *Catalogue*, no. 689.
Acquired by Henry Walters (?) before 1931. (48.1562)

In this tiny baboon made of faience, the characteristic features of the standard Egyptian representation are exaggerated. Seated with his hands drawn up on his knees, the baboon is nearly enveloped by a solid mass of hair. The hair is perforated behind the ears.

Cat. no. 13

Cat. no. 14

Cat. no. 15

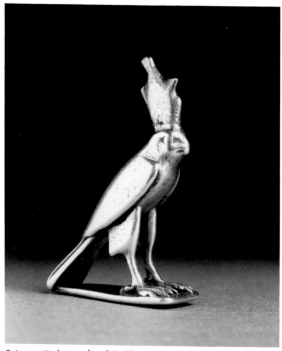

Cat. no. 17 (see colorplate II)

15

Snake Amulet

Egyptian, n.d.
Length: 1¼ in. (3.2 cm)
Acquired by Henry Walters (?) before 1931. (42.357)

This carnelian amulet represents the upper body and head of a snake. The eyes are indicated by incision. The piece was designed to be worn on the neck of a mummy.

Notes: For a discussion of the type, see I. E. S. Edwards, *Tutankhamun's Jewelry,* The Metropolitan Museum of Art, 1976, no. 21, p. 38f (the underside of the snake is illustrated there).

16

Pendant

Egyptian, n.d.
Height: 1⅝ in. (4.1 cm)
Publications: Steindorff, *Catalogue,* no. 670, pl. C.
Purchased by Henry Walters, 1913. (42.224)

In this heavy-breasted falcon carved of lapis lazuli, only the general forms, the round eyes, and the line across the beak are presented. There is a peculiar sharply cut depression behind the head, which suggests a ruff.

Horus, the great Egyptian national god, could also be represented as a falcon, and amulets representing him, such as this example and the one that follows (Cat. no. 17), occur in all periods, materials, and techniques.

17

Pendant

Egyptian, n.d.
Height: 1½ in. (3.8 cm)
Publications: Steindorff, *Catalogue,* no. 676.
Acquired by Henry Walters (?) before 1931. (57.1433)

This solid-gold falcon wears a double crown of silver. Traces of chased lines in the eye area and wedge-shaped indentations on the body (best preserved on the upper right leg) suggest that details were originally indicated. A loop for suspension is attached to the bird's left shoulder.

18

Pendant

Egyptian, n.d.
Height: 1 1/16 in. (2.7 cm)
Publications: Steindorff, *Catalogue,* no. 531.
Purchased by Henry Walters, 1913. (42.344)

Finely carved of green and white jasper, this tiny pendant represents Onuris, god of the atmosphere and a god of war. The facial features and hair are done in relief, the feathers of the crown by incision.

19

Ring

Egyptian, Late Middle Kingdom, ca. 1700 B.C.
Diameter: 1 3/16 in. (3.0 cm)
Length of bezel: 7/8 in. (2.2 cm)
Publications: Geoffry T. Martin, *Egyptian Administrative and Private-name Seals,* Oxford, 1971, p. 38, no. 425, pls. 11, 38 (with a different reading).
Gift of the children of Robert Garrett, 1964. (57.1957)

One of the earliest rings in the collection, this is a good example of a characteristic Egyptian type. A rock crystal scarab with base and sides covered with thin sheet gold is attached to the sockets of a tapered hoop by a thick gold wire that runs through the scarab. Chased on the gold base is an inscription that may be translated, "Butler of Nefer-Her (the beautiful of face) Heby," suggesting that the piece belonged to a royal butler.

20

Ring Bezel

Egyptian, Twelfth Dynasty (twentieth-eighteenth century B.C.)
Length: 15/16 in. (2.4 cm)
Purchased by Henry Walters, 1913. (42.38)

Made of turquoise-colored glazed steatite and perforated longitudinally, this scarab was probably once mounted as a ring. The elaborate gold frame around the bottom was made of thick sheet gold to which two strands of twisted gold wire flanking notched gold wire were added. The free movement of the interlocking scroll pattern carved into the base of the scarab witnesses the influence of Cretan art.

Cat. no. 18

Cat. no. 19

Cat. no. 19

Cat. no. 20

Cat. no. 20

Cat. no. 21

21
Ring

Egyptian, 1379-1362 B.C.
Diameter: 7/8 in. (2.2 cm)
Length of bezel: 11/16 in. (1.8 cm)
Purchased by Henry Walters from Maurice Nahman, 1929. (57.1471)

This heavy gold signet ring with a stirrup-shaped hoop was cast in a single piece, the deeper part of the hieroglyphs having been cut into the wax model. Some details of the signs were chased later. The surface shows much wear. The hieroglyphs read *Nefer-kheperu-re'-wa'-en-Re'*—the throne name of King Amenhotep IV (Akhenaten).

22
Ring with Giant Bezel

Egyptian, tenth-eighth century B.C.
Diameter: 3/4 in. (1.9 cm)
Length of bezel: 2 9/16 in. (6.5 cm)
Purchased by Henry Walters, 1929. (42.418)

The surface within the signs of this greenish faience ring is well preserved and bluer than the rest of the ring. The inscription may be translated, "He who is on the seat of Amun-Re'-Kamutef." This god was honored in a special cult at Karnak.

This type of cartouche-shaped faience signet ring with a very long bezel was popular from the late Twen-tieth Dynasty to the Twenty-third Dynasty (1000-730 B.C.). A question exists as to whether these rings were ever actually used as signets. They might have been religious souvenirs, gifts for special occasions, or items of funerary jewelry. It seems probable that rings with blank bezels were mass-made in molds and that before

Cat. no. 22

firing, while the material was soft, the inscription was added.

Notes: For a discussion of the dates for such rings, see William C. Hayes, *The Hyksos Period and The New Kingdom (1675-1080 B.C.),* The Scepter of Egypt, A Background for the Study of the Egyptian Antiquities in the Metropolitan Museum of Art, Part II, Cambridge, Massachusetts, 1959, p. 397, fig. 250.

23
Frog Ring

Egyptian, n.d.
Diameter: ⅝ in. (1.6 cm)
Length of frog: ¼ in. (.6 cm)
Acquired by Henry Walters (?) before 1931. (42.1470)

A tiny well-modeled frog sits on the rectangular bezel of this carnelian ring in which the "end" of the hoop is carved to imitate a cup-fastener. The gold inner facing may be modern.

Because frogs seem to be self created—born magically from the mud in which they live—they became in earliest times symbols of birth and resurrection and of

the birth goddess, Heket. Frogs were also used as a sign in the hieroglyphic script, sometimes as an ideogram for "repeating life."

Notes: For frogs see Alan H. Gardiner, *Egyptian Grammar; Being an Introduction to the Study of Hieroglyphics,* Oxford, 1927, 1, no. 7; Ingrid Gamer-Wallert, *Fische und Fischkulte im alten Ägypten. Ägyptologische Abhandlungen* 21 (eds. Wolfgang Helck, Eberhard Otto), Wiesbaden, 1970, p. 124; for a gold ring with a frog bezel from the Amarna period (fourteenth century B.C.), see Aldred, *Jewels,* colorplate 69.

24
Amulets for Mummy Wrappings

Egyptian, Late period (seventh-fourth century B.C.)
Scarab: height 1⅝ in. (4.1 cm), width 1¼ in. (3.2 cm)
Wings: height 1¼ in. (3.2 cm), width 2⅝ in. (6.7 cm)
Jackals of Anubis: heights 1¹³/₁₆ in. and 1¾ in. (4.6 cm and 4.5 cm), widths 2⅛ in. and 1⅞ in. (5.4 cm and 4.8 cm)
Isis: height 2¼ in. (5.7 cm), width 1¹/₁₆ in. (2.7 cm)
Nephythys: height 2⅛ in. (5.4 cm), width 1⅜ in. (3.5 cm)
Jackal-head plaque: height 3⅝ in. (9.2 cm)
Falcon-head plaque: height 3½ in. (8.9 cm)
Human-head plaque: height 3⁹/₁₆ in. (9.1 cm)
Baboon-head plaque: height 3½ in. (8.9 cm)
Acquired by Henry Walters (?) before 1931. (42.373, 48.1667-68, 48.1634-37, 48.1638-41, 48.2052)

Typical sets of faience amulets such as are found sewn on mummy wrappings are arranged here on a reconstructed net of beads of the kind used to cover mummies. At the top is a winged scarab, beneath which is a set of relief plaques, the outer ones representing the jackal of Anubis on his shrine and the inner ones representing Isis at left and Nephythys at right. The four mummiform plaques around the sides are made of painted faience. They represent the four sons of Horus with heads of a jackal, falcon, human, and baboon.

Cat. no. 23

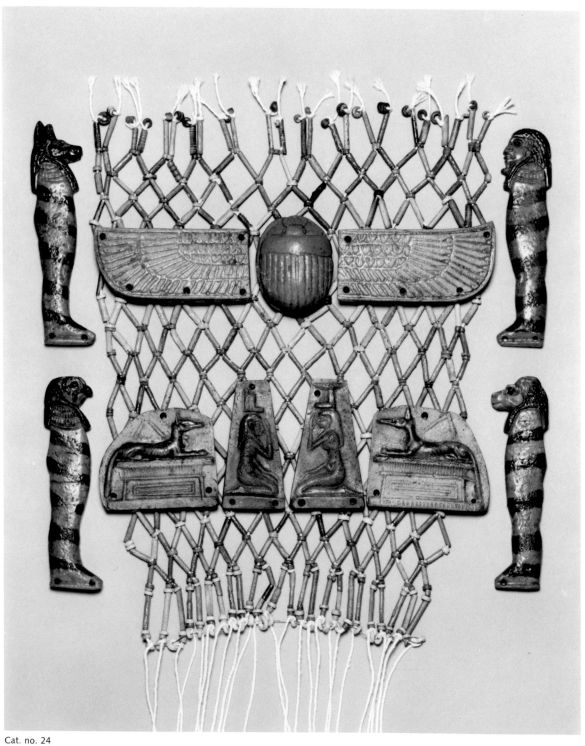

Cat. no. 24

Etruscan Jewelry

Etruscan civilization, already at an advanced level both technically and artistically by 700 B.C., has long been an enigma to scholars, and it is unlikely that we will ever be certain of its origins. Because the Etruscans left few written records, we depend on the observations of Greek and Roman historians and on the evidence of archaeology, which is neither profuse nor always precise. Otto Brendel in his book *Etruscan Art* (New York, 1979) offers the following thoughts on the development of the Etruscan civilization and artistic style. About 800 B.C. the native "Villanovan" population of central Italy migrated suddenly to the coastal areas of Etruria. The reasons for this are unknown, but the result was a vast increase in trade and contact with other areas of the ancient world. The artistic style that we call Etruscan was thus formed from the crosscurrents of several contemporary civilizations, Syrian, Phoenician, and Greek among them.

A large portion of the Etruscan jewelry shown here dates to the earliest period of Etruscan art, about 700-625 B.C. Made with great technical skill, the jewelry of this period is difficult to duplicate even with modern tools. The most important decorative technique was granulation, examples of which are the necklace sections (Cat. nos. 31, 32), and throughout this period Eastern motifs and types abound: note the Syrian winged bulls, sphinxes, and women with long volute locks on the *mitra* relief (Cat. no. 25).

At the end of the seventh century B.C. and during the following century, Greek artistic traditions gradually became dominant in Etruscan art. Greece had also been strongly infused with Eastern traditions during the late eighth and seventh centuries B.C.; and by the end of the seventh century B.C., the Eastern elements had been assimilated. On jewelry decorative floral elements such as palmettes and rosettes, although ultimately of Eastern origin, come via Greece. Note the palmettes on the necklace pendants (Cat. no. 30).

The Walters is fortunate in possessing a masterpiece of fifth-century B.C. Etruscan jewelry, the Daedalus bulla (Cat. no. 38). Bearing an inscription in the Etruscan alphabet, the bulla is one of a very few pieces of inscribed jewelry from this period.

Late Etruscan jewelry is considered to have been made beginning about 400 B.C., when filigree and granulation give way to large gold surfaces, often worked in repoussé. This period is sparsely represented at the Walters, but the hoop earring (Cat. no. 27) may date to the early fourth century B.C.

In the third century B.C. jewelry that can be called specifically Etruscan is supplanted in Italy by jewelry that is essentially Hellenistic, a pan-Mediterranean style with local variations.

Etruscan jewelry can be dated on the basis of comparisons with tomb groups found in Etruria; however, this process has a large margin of error because most tombs were "excavated" by treasure hunters rather than by archaeologists. Furthermore, items found in the same tomb cannot be assumed to date to the same time. Not only might objects such as jewelry be heirlooms treasured for several generations, but tombs were reused for successive burials for as long as a century. One of the most famous Etruscan tombs, the Regolini-Galassi tomb at Cervetri, illustrates some of the problems faced.

The tomb was opened in the spring of 1836 by two men looking primarily for gold and silver treasure—the Vicar of Cervetri, Alessandro Regolini, and his partner, General Vincenzo Galassi. Afraid of tomb robbers, they removed all the precious metal objects in the tomb as quickly as possible, ignoring the bones of the dead as well as most of the pottery and keeping no day-by-day account of their activity. Most of the finds were removed first to Galassi's house and ultimately to the Vatican, where they are today. A few have turned up in other museums, and one object from the tomb, an ivory pyxis picked up forty years after the discovery of the tomb by the vicar of the parish, even made its way to the Walters Art Gallery. Summary records kept by the excavators and reports by several visitors list the objects and where they were found, but the accounts vary and the actual disposition of the goods in the grave cannot now be ascertained.

The tomb consisted of an antechamber, with niches on either side, divided from an inner chamber by a stone bench. Most of the written accounts and the nature of the finds themselves suggest that there were a series of burials made over a long period: in the inner chamber, a woman buried with a wealth of gold jewelry; in the antechamber, a warrior laid out on a bed, with chariot and weapons nearby; and in the right-hand niche, a cremation.

A few fragments of Proto-Corinthian vases, *skyphoi* and *oinochoai*, suggest that the latest date for burial in the tomb is 625 B.C. Of the finds said to have come from the inner chamber, Cypro-Phoenician silver bowls and silver jugs imported from the Near East indicate a date in the first half of the seventh century for the woman's burial.

From the character of the finds and the records of their distribution, it is possible to tell something about the people buried in the tomb. The woman's burial was the richest. (Inscriptions on several vases may give her name—Larthia.) Her burial included silver and bronze vessels and a rich assortment of gold jewelry, several pieces of which are very much like examples at the Walters.

Because none of the Etruscan jewelry in the Walters' collection has an established provenance, finds from the Regolini-Galassi tomb and others like it provide the only evidence for dating the jewelry and establishing where it might have been made and what it was used for.

Diana M. Buitron

25

Gold Sheet Relief: *Mitra*

Etruscan, ca. 700 B.C.
Height: 2⅝ in. (6.7 cm)
Width: 4⅞ in. (12.4 cm)
Publications: Strøm, *Etruscan Orientalizing Style*, cat.
no. 59, pp. 77-79, 207-208, fig. 39.
Acquired by Henry Walters from Joseph Brummer,
1927. (57.369)

This *mitra* (head or belt ornament) consists of a roughly
semicircular sheet divided into three zones separated
by rows of dots, with a border of hatched triangles
along the semicircular edge and four rows of dots along
the top. Most of the figures in the two upper zones
were probably worked individually, rather than
stamped. In the top zone are three winged bulls. Above
each bull is a head, and under the center bull there are
three heads. Between the bulls are standing women
with long volute locks and transparent garments. On
the left and right are pairs of goats. In the middle zone
are two winged bulls (opposed), four ducks beneath,
four double leaf ornaments, four circle ornaments, and
two quadrupeds (perhaps sphinxes), one in each upper
corner. In the bottom zone is a procession of lions and
goats. The lions, goats, heads, ducks, and circles are
the results of stamps struck while the gold sheet was
placed face down in a substance such as pitch. The
edges of the sheet are frayed and crumpled. Along the
top the metal is rolled back in three places, perhaps to
form tubes for suspension.

Notes: Ingrid Strøm has placed this *mitra* in her group of South
Etruscan jewelry reliefs, somewhat Orientalizing in style, dated to
around and shortly after the year 700 B.C. To place these reliefs in a

Cat. no. 25 (see colorplate IV)

relative stylistic chronology, Dr. Strøm chooses certain recurring motifs as the criteria: here, the "plump duck" is the significant motif. Furthermore, the two main zones on the *mitra* show a certain freedom and development in composition and style, rather than the strict division into friezes seen on earlier Geometric examples.

26

Gold Leech Earring

Etruscan, sixth-fourth century B.C.
Height: 13/16 in. (2.1 cm)
Collection of Henry Walters, before 1931; Mrs. Henry Walters; purchased from Joseph Brummer, 1941.
(57.1678)

This gold leech earring is made of a single sheet rolled into a tubular hoop. The seam is visible on the inner face. The outer face is decorated with half globules bordered on the sides and ends with twisted wire. The back portion of the hoop is undecorated. Suspended below are four globules, each dotted with three granules.

Its resemblance to the bloodsucking annelid worm gives this earring its modern name. The type, which goes back to the Middle Bronze Age in Crete, survived in Cyprus through the Dark Ages and reappeared in Sicily and Greece in the seventh and sixth centuries B.C. Generally made of one or more sheets joined to form a tubular hoop decorated with granules, globules, and filigree, leech earrings were secured by a wire that actually pierced the flesh.

Notes: Compare an earring from a fourth-century tomb at Praeneste (A. Pasqui, "Palestrina," *NSc*, 1897, p. 263, fig. 5) and an earring in London (*BMCJ*, no. 2245).

27

Hoop Earring

Etruscan, probably fourth century B.C.
Diameter: 1 1/16 in. (2.7 cm)
Collection of Henry Walters, before 1931; Mrs. Henry Walters; purchased from Joseph Brummer, 1941.
(57.1673)

This gold hoop and pendant probably served as the pendant of an earring. Attached to the hoop, which is solid bronze overlaid with gold leaf, is a small gold bulla, its top formed by a tube decorated with filigree and edged by tiny tubes that spiral where they touch the bulla. The bulla swivels and can lie either within or without the hollow of the hoop.

Hoop earrings are a major type of Etruscan earring. Based on a tubular hoop, their simplest form is a wire hoop with the ends crossed over and wound around each other. In its early variations one end of the earring might flare out like a trumpet or have an animal's head on it. Later, one end of the hoop has a hollow bead, and in the most elaborate types a hoop and pendant like the example shown here might be added to the basic hoop.

Notes: See Alexander, *Jewelry*, p. 23, fig. 76; Becatti, *Oreficerie*, pl. CX, no. 414; and Hadaczek, *Ohrschmuck*, p. 65.

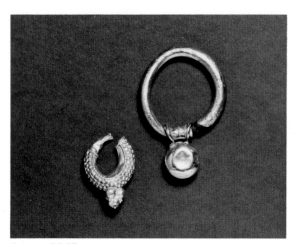

Cat. nos. 26, 27

Cat. nos. 28, 29

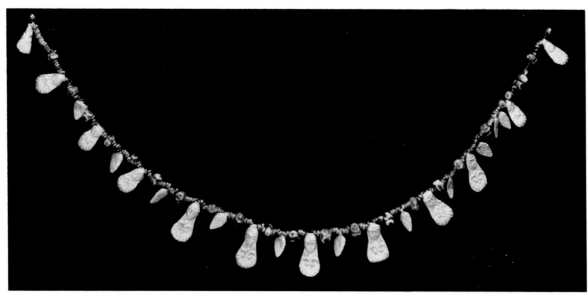

Cat. no. 30 (see colorplate V)

28
Spirals

Etruscan, seventh century B.C.
Diameter: 7/16 in. (1.1 cm)
Height: 5/16 in. (.8 cm)
Acquired by Henry Walters from Joseph Brummer,
1927. (57.417-18)

These gold spirals reverse direction in the center, forming a loop. The loop and ends are flattened and have
oblong strips attached. The strips on the ends of each
spiral are ornamented with a row of nine globules,
followed by a hollow hemisphere that was once filled
with glass or paste and a tenth globule. The strip on the
central loop is similar, but the hollow hemisphere is
replaced with a dark stone, perhaps glass, set in a ring
of twisted wire.

   Spirals such as these and the one that follows (Cat.
no. 29) are especially common in seventh-century
Etruscan tombs and may be made of gold, silver, or
bronze. Their use is not known for certain: earring
pendants, hair ornaments, and children's rings are the
usual suggestions. Some are quite ornate, often ending
in heads of animals or humans; others are simply plain
gold wire.

Notes: Compare *BMCJ*, pl. XVI, no. 1329.

29
Spiral

Etruscan, seventh century B.C.
Diameter: 3/8 in. (1.0 cm)
Height: 9/16 in. (1.4 cm)
Collection of Henry Walters before 1931; Mrs. Henry
Walters; purchased from Joseph Brummer, 1941.
(57.1631)

A narrow gold strip flattened on the inside and rounded
on the outside, this spiral is coiled three times to form a
serpent. Details of the head and scales at both ends are
chased.

30
Necklace

Etruscan, seventh-sixth century B.C.
Diameter of zinc beads: 1/8 in. (.3 cm)
Diameter of glass beads: 1/4 in. (.6 cm)
Heights of pendants: 7/8 in. (2.2 cm), 11/16 in. (1.8 cm),
1/2 in. (1.3 cm)
Collection of Henry Walters before 1931; Mrs. Henry
Walters; purchased from Joseph Brummer, 1941.
(57.1676)

This necklace includes two hundred two cylindrical zinc
beads; twenty-three glass beads, white and blue on

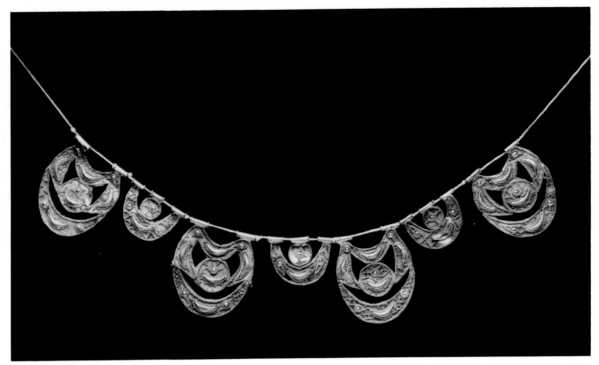

Cat. nos. 31, 32

dark blue; and twenty-three gold relief pendants, each made of a single sheet worked in repoussé. Twelve of the pendants represent human heads with palmettes; eleven depict bunches of grapes.

A great variety in shape, size, and decoration was possible in Etruscan necklaces and bracelets. The arrangement of pendants (ornaments with pipes or rings for suspension) and beads (ornaments that are themselves pierced for suspension) of the necklace shown here is—like most combinations of necklace elements —a reconstruction, but it gives an idea of how a necklace might have looked. In the examples that follow (Cat. nos. 31-35), pendants and beads are illustrated separately but can be imagined in various combinations.

Notes: Similar relief heads on palmettes are known from the graves of La Pietrera at Vetulonia, dated to the late seventh century B.C. (Randall-MacIver, *Villanovans*, pls. 2, 29). The silver pendants of the rectangular relief, no. 175, are also very similar. Similar glass beads are found on three necklaces in London (*BMCJ*, pl. XXI, nos. 1450, 1452, pl. XXIII, no. 1454). Zinc beads do not yet appear to be known for this period.

31
Necklace Sections

Etruscan, seventh-sixth century B.C.
Height: 9/16 in. (1.4 cm)
Width: ¾ in. (1.9 cm)
Acquired by Henry Walters from Joseph Brummer, 1927. (57.408)

Three necklace sections, strung here with four larger sections (Cat. no. 32), are made of a sheet of gold cut to form a crescent and a circle. The sections are decorated with applied circles and crescents and granulation design with variations. There are three suspension pipes on each section. The crescents, circles, and pipes are edged with twisted wire.

Notes: Crescents and circles in a slightly different configuration, but similarly decorated, are found on a necklace in the Metropolitan Museum of Art dated to the eighth-seventh century B.C. (Alexander, *Jewelry*, fig. 3).

32

Necklace Sections

Etruscan, seventh-sixth century B.C.
Height: 1⅛ in. (2.9 cm)
Width: 1¹/₁₆ in. (2.7 cm)
Acquired by Henry Walters from Joseph Brummer, 1927. (57.406)

Each of these four necklace sections is made of a sheet of gold cut to form four crescents and a circle. The sections are decorated with applied raised crescents and circles and granulation design. Each section has suspension pipes at the top and two additional pipes on the back. The crescents, circles, and suspension pipes are edged with twisted wire.

Cat. no. 33

33

Pendant

Etruscan, seventh-sixth century B.C.
Height: 1 in. (2.5 cm)
Acquired by Henry Walters from Joseph Brummer, 1927. (57.488)

This pendant is of gold leaf over a silver core. The gold leaf is missing from the suspension ring and from the bottom. The two sides have the same intricate design made with granules.

34

Gold Beads

Etruscan, seventh-sixth century B.C.
Diameter: ⅜ in. (1.0 cm)
Acquired by Henry Walters from Joseph Brummer, 1927. (57.461)

Each of these eight hollow rounded beads, open at both ends, is made of one sheet bent to form a sphere. A smooth wire is placed around the openings on seven of the beads (missing on the eighth).

Cat. no. 34

35

Gold Beads

Etruscan, seventh-sixth century B.C.
Diameters: ¼ in. and ⅛ in.(.6 cm and .3 cm)
Acquired by Henry Walters from Joseph Brummer, 1927. (57.405)

Twelve of these sixteen gold beads are hollow and round with eight granules edging each opening. The four smaller beads are biconical and have seven granules at each opening.

Cat. no. 35

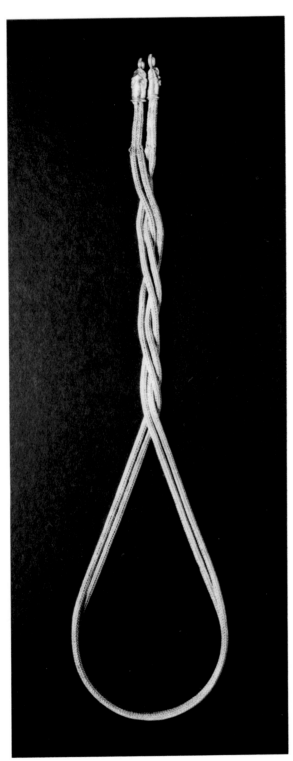

Cat. no. 36

36

Gold Necklace

Etruscan, seventh century B.C.
Length of necklace: 26½ in. (67.3 cm)
Length of finials: $^{13}/_{16}$ in. (2.1 cm)
Acquired by Henry Walters from Joseph Brummer, 1927. (57.458)

A thick rope braid composed of eight pairs of wires twisted together and laid side by side is capped on either end by lion-head finials with loops in their gaping jaws. The lions' heads are cast. The loops were probably made separately.

Notes: A similar necklace composed of a thick rope braid and ending in double lion-head finials and loops was found in the Regolini-Galassi tomb at Cervetri and dated to the mid-seventh century B.C. (Pareti, *Regolini-Galassi*, pl. V; and Higgins, *Greek and Roman Jewellery*, p. 214). This type of necklace continues in use, the plaited rope replaced with complex chains, into the Hellenistic period (Alexander, *Jewelry*, p. 6). For the technique of the plaited rope, see Hoffmann and Davidson, *Greek Gold*, p. 37.

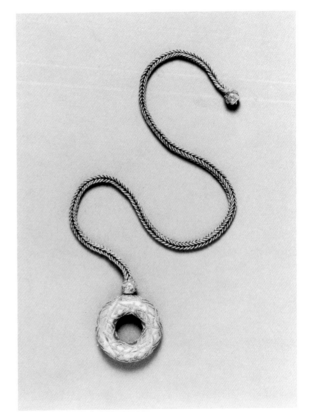

Cat. no. 37

37

Gold Ornament on a Rope Braid

Etruscan, seventh century B.C.
Length of braid: 6⅞ in. (17.5 cm)
Diameter of tube: ¹¹/₁₆ in. (1.8 cm)
Diameter of beads: ³/₁₆ in. (.5 cm)
Acquired by Henry Walters from Joseph Brummer,
1927. (57.410)

The hollow gold tube on this rope braid is decorated
with lozenges and zigzags of granulation. The braid is
composed of four pairs of wires twisted together and
laid side by side. At each end of the braid is a bead
decorated with triangles of granulation and edged by
smooth wire. The frayed ends of one end of the braid
indicate that it was once longer. The join of the braid to
the tube is probably modern.

Cat. no. 38

38

Gold Bulla

Etruscan, first half of fifth century B.C.
Height overall: 1⁹/₁₆ in. (4.0 cm)
Height without stopper: 1³/₁₆ in. (3.0 cm)
Width: 1 in. (2.5 cm)
Publications: Franz Messerschmidt, Review of V.
Dumitrescu, L'Età del Ferro nel Piceno, in *Gnomon* 9,
1933, p. 161; George M. A. Hanfmann, "Daidalos in
Etruria," *AJA* 39, 1935, pp. 189-94, pl. XXV; Eva Fiesel,
"The Inscription on the Etruscan Bulla," *AJA* 39, 1935,
pp. 195-97; John D. Beazley, "Groups of Early Black
Figures," *Hesperia* 13, 1944, p. 9, 43; Arvid Andrén,
"Oreficerie e plastica etrusca," *Opuscula Archaeolo-
gica* 5, 1948, p. 94, fig. 6; Becatti, *Oreficerie*, p. 186,
no. 316, pl. 78; Emeline H. Richardson, *The Etruscans,
Their Art and Civilization*, Chicago, 1964, pp. 152 ff.,
pl. XLa; Frank Brommer, *Denkmälerlisten zu griechis-
chen Heldensagen*, 3rd ed., Marburg, 1976, p. 63;
Cleveland Museum of Art, *Exhibition of Gold*, October
31, 1947-January 11, 1948; Dayton Art Institute,
Flight: Fantasy, Faith, Fact, December 17, 1953-
February 21, 1954, no. 138; The Detroit Institute of
Arts, *Ancient Italic and Etruscan Art*, January 15-
February 23, 1958; Worcester Art Museum, *Master-
pieces of Etruscan Art*, Worcester, April 21-June 4,
1967, no. 56, text by R. S. Teitz.

Said to be from Comacchio, near Ferrara; purchased by
Henry Walters from Sangiorgi, 1930. (57.371)

This elaborate and beautiful bulla (a hollow pendant
that could contain perfume or a charm) depicts the
mythical craftsman Daedalus on one side and his ill-
fated son Icarus on the other. Retrograde Etruscan
inscriptions name the figures as *Vikare* (Icarus) and
Taitle (Daedalus). Daedalus carries a saw and adze,
implements he is said to have invented (Pliny, *Natural
History*, VII, 198). Icarus carries a draftsman's square
and a double axe, more properly attributes of his
father. Both figures are shown flying—wings spread
and legs drawn up. The contour of the wings and heads
is the line along which the sheets that form the bulla are
joined. The figures are worked in repoussé, and the
details are chased and incised. Around the base and
neck are circles of twisted wire. The suspension handles
are formed of a hollow hoop and a circle of twisted
wire. The stopper has a central hoop with twisted wire
on either side and at the ends. A cord or flexible chain
would have passed through the handles and stopper
for suspending the container around the neck or arm.

The stopper could be removed by simply lifting it, and snapped back into place by releasing the chain.

The bulla is an Etruscan ornament in general use from the fifth century B.C. onwards, later adopted by the Romans. The story of Daedalus and Icarus, a favorite subject in antiquity, is represented on this bulla in a very early, if not the earliest, stage. The style suggests a date in the first half of the fifth century B.C. The contents remaining inside were tested and found to include traces of labdanum, a substance used to fix scents.

39
Gold and Bone Pin

Etruscan, seventh century B.C.
Length: 4^{1}/16 in. (10.3 cm)
Diameter of globe: ^{5}/16 in. (.8 cm)
Acquired by Henry Walters from Joseph Brummer, 1927. (57.471)

The hollow gold globe of this pin is made in two parts, with five granules on top and a collar with settings for two granules or gems edged by smooth wires. The shaft is made of bone.

Since Etruscan dress, like that of the Greeks, generally involved a length of material folded around the body, fasteners such as this pin and the one that follows (Cat. no. 40) played a most important role. Representations on sculpture and on vases show pairs of pins used at the shoulders or single pins attaching cloaks.

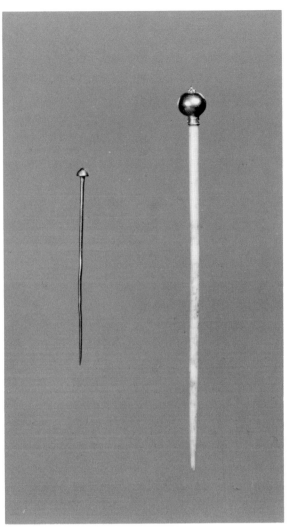

Cat. nos. 39, 40

40

Gold Pin

Etruscan, seventh century B.C.
Length: 2⅛ in. (5.4 cm)
Acquired by Henry Walters from Joseph Brummer,
1927. (57.474)

This gold pin consists of a spherical cap attached to a
straight shaft.

Greek Jewelry

Greek literature makes it clear that jewelry played an important role both as adornment and as a sign of wealth from Homeric times on. Book XIV of the *Iliad* tells us that when Hera dressed up to seduce Zeus, she put on an embroidered robe fastened with gold pins and a pair of earrings with three clustering drops. Penelope's suitors in the *Odyssey,* Book XVII, vying with one another to win her hand, offered such gifts as a necklace, earrings, a robe with twelve gold pins, and a cunningly wrought chain strung with amber beads.

That certain jewels also had magical properties, an idea that stems from the Near East, is confirmed by Pliny who tells us that the Herakles knot, often used as the centerpiece of diadems, had the power of healing wounds. The representation of the Isis crown (see Cat. no. 43) is an allusion to a popular Egyptian cult.

Like Etruscan jewelry, Greek jewelry was made for use both in life and death. Ancient representations of women at their toilette show the kind of jewelry a well-dressed woman would wear: a diadem, earrings, a necklace, bracelets, and rings. Favorite ornaments were buried with their owner, and most of the jewelry we have today was preserved in tombs.

The Homeric descriptions of a wealth of gold jewelry may reflect the actual situation in the Bronze Age civilizations of Crete and Mycenae. The gold signet ring engraved with a battle scene (Cat. no. 41) is similar to examples found in the shaft graves at Mycenae and comes from this early period.

About 1100 B.C., when the Mycenaean world collapsed, a period of poverty lasting nearly four centuries was ushered in; and during this time jewelry was extremely scarce. These "Dark Ages" began to lighten during the eighth century B.C., when contacts between Greece and the more prosperous East were intensified.

During the seventh and sixth centuries B.C. many new types and techniques appear. The gold and sard scarab ring (Cat. no. 50) is an example of an Egyptian type that became popular throughout the Mediterranean world.

By the fifth century B.C., after the Persian wars, exploitation of the silver mines of Laurion and the gold mines at Mount Pangaeus created a period of prosperity. This affluence is recorded by Xenophon, writing in the early part of the fourth century B.C., who says that Athenian men spent their wealth on armor, horses, and houses, while the women went in for expensive clothes and gold jewelry (*Ways and Means,* IV, 8).

Perhaps as a result of this eager market, goldsmiths' work from the Classical period on was recognized as a medium for high artistic achievement. Jewelry of this period demonstrates that realistic sculpture in the round was possible on a miniature scale. Alexander the Great (356-323 B.C.) had his portrait carved in an emerald, and this gave impetus to the fashion for portrait gemstones. An example of this type shows the head of the wine god Dionysos (Cat. no. 52).

After the conquests of Alexander, the Greek world included Egypt, Syria, Cyprus, and much of Asia Minor, as well as Persia. The capture of the Treasure of Darius by Alexander's troops resulted in the dissemination of many new motifs and, more importantly, in the increased use of inlaid stones, glass, and enamel, setting the scene for the development of the Roman jewelry style.

We know that during the Hellenistic period important jewelry centers were located at Tarentum, Alexandria, and Antioch, each of which must have produced distinctive types of ornaments. Unfortunately, the exact origin of most of the classical jewelry in the Walters' collection can only be surmised. One exception is the Hellenistic ring (Cat. no. 52) said to be from Tarsus. The wide range of types and styles suggests something of the richness and variety of Greek jewelry and indicates the degree of prosperity and elegance that Greek civilization attained.

Diana M. Buitron

Cat. no. 41

41

Signet Ring

Mycenaean, 1500-1200 B.C.
Diameter: $^{13}/_{16}$ in. (2.1 cm)
Length of bezel: 1$^1/_{16}$ in. (2.7 cm)
Purchased from Arthur Sambon, Paris, 1926. (57.1006)

The hollow hoop of this ring, which is flat on the inside and convex on the outside, is worked in repoussé to form a central ridge. The oval bezel is formed of two sheets of gold—the upper decorated, the lower concave to accommodate the finger—seamed together and applied transversely to the hoop. The intaglio decoration, which has been either driven in with punches or beaten over a mold (the details then engraved), is a battle scene. The warrior on the left has fallen back on his right knee and holds up his shield for protection against the warrior attacking from the right who brandishes a spear in his left hand. On the right is a quiver and two palm branches; above and below, a rouletted border.

Signet rings were popular from the sixteenth century B.C. onwards. Their practical use as identifying marks pressed into soft clay or wax does not seem to have been as important as their ornamental use, since generally the compositions are shown in the natural, rather than the reverse, direction.

Notes: The type is known in Crete, but this ring finds its closest comparison in rings from Mycenaean Greece (*CMS*, vol. 1, nos. 16, 127 [from Mycenae], no. 219 [from the Vaphio Tomb]; see also John Boardman, *Greek Gems and Finger Rings*, London, 1970, pl. 153).

42

Earring with Head of Black

Greek, third century B.C.
Height without loop: $^9/_{16}$ in. (1.4 cm)
Acquired before 1931. (57.1562)

A negroid head, probably garnet, is set between a rosette-cup base and a cap of gold hair. The eyes are drilled and were once inlaid with colored glass. A gold pin runs through the head and cap and forms a suspension loop on top. The rosette at the base has a granule center and twisted wire petals. The cap of hair appears to have been made of wire coils, which have been worn or polished almost smooth. The earring, which is one of a pair, shows signs of a modern repair at the base. The Greeks had long been fascinated by the peoples of Africa and represented them in every medium.

Notes: For the head and the rosette-cup base, parallels in ancient times exist—most from Etruria of the third century B.C. (Hackens, *Classical Jewelry*, no. 7). To Hackens' list of examples of the type can be added a group of similar earrings (also of the third century B.C.) from Yugoslavia (V. Bitrakova, ''Zlatni Nakit iz Helenističke Nekropole kod Crevejnce,'' *Archeološki Radovi I Rasprave* 4-5, Zagreb, 1967, pl. I).

Cat. no. 42

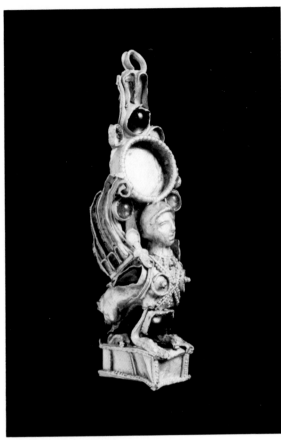

Cat. no. 43 (see colorplate VI)

43

Earring Pendant: Sphinx

Greek, second-first century B.C.
Height: 1¹⁵/₁₆ in. (4.9 cm)
Width: ½ in. (1.3 cm)
Acquired before 1931. (57.1490)

This gold pendant consists of three elements: base, sphinx, and headdress. The trapezoidal base is made of three sheets of metal for the top, sides, and bottom. The joins are masked with twisted and smooth wires, the sides by wire colonnettes. The crouching sphinx is hollow, worked in repoussé, and adorned with a necklace and double bandoliers made of smooth and twisted wire and rows and clusters of granules. Below the breast is a rectangular box setting for a garnet. The

legs are strips of metal separately applied. The wings, also separately applied, consist of several sheets of metal of different shapes—the edges raised to hold stones or enamel inlays—placed close together to resemble feathers. Only one of the inlaid stones is preserved—a garnet on the sphinx's right wing. The wings are supported in back by a tubular strut that runs between them. The headdress, a large round setting for a stone (now missing), is flanked by four smaller settings (garnets preserved in the lower two), above which is an Isis crown consisting of a round setting with garret-shaped settings. The feathers and disk headdress, or Isis crown, appear frequently in jewelry of the second-first century B.C. in the eastern Mediterranean.

Notes: Sphinxes seated on pedestals are known from Theodosia, Crimea, (*ABC,* pl. XII a, 2); Amphipolis, Northern Greece, (*BCH,* vol. 83, 1959, p. 710, fig. 2); and Kerch, South Russia, (Gleb Sokolov, *Antique Art on the Northern Black Sea Coast,* Leningrad, 1974, p. 45, no. 26); but none are as elaborate as the Walters' example. The lavish inlay accords with a date in the second-first century B.C.

44

Hoop Earring: Lion's Head

Greek, fourth-third century B.C.
Height: ¾ in. (1.9 cm)
Acquired before 1931. (57.581)

Four hollow tapering gold wires, spirally wound around each other, narrow at one end to form the pin of the earring and widen at the other end to fit into a collar of seven leaves chased to resemble a lion's mane. The wires are encircled by plain and twisted wires. The lion's head is worked in repoussé and chased. The eyes and ears are hollowed out, and the mouth has a hole in the center for attaching the pin.

Hoop earrings with animal-head finials, such as this example, which is one of a pair, and those following (Cat. nos. 45, 46), originated in Greece at the time of Alexander the Great, about 330 B.C. They may have developed from a simple tapered hoop with a knob finial at the larger end, a type known in Macedonia as early as the fifth century B.C. With Alexander's conquests, the repertory of motifs opened up, and the variety of animals' heads is evidence of the eclectic nature of Hellenistic art.

The hoop is generally either formed of coiled wires or worked in repoussé (sometimes elaborated with thin twisted wires) to give the impression of coiled wires (see Cat. no. 46). The hoop may also consist of a flaring tube spirally wound with wire (see Cat. no. 45), or it may be left plain. The point of the tapering end was thrust through the earlobe into the loop at the animal's head. The animal's head could be worn upside down or right side up. Lions' heads are the most common finials on hoop earrings. Many examples can be cited, most dated by tomb groups to the fourth-third centuries B.C.

Notes: For the type see Higgins, *Greek and Roman Jewellery*, p. 162.

45

Hoop Earring: Lions' Heads

Western Greek, fourth-third century B.C.
Height: $^{13}/_{16}$ in. (2.1 cm)
Collection of Henry Walters before 1931; Mrs. Henry Walters; purchased from Joseph Brummer, 1941. (57.1665)

This hoop consists of plain wire wound around a tapering gold core that terminates in large and small lions' heads. The small lion's head holds a thin wire in its mouth that hooks into the loop held by the large lion's head. Both heads are worked in repoussé and chased. The inlaid eyes of the large head are missing, and the small head has been crushed. The collar of the small head is a plain tube; that of the large head is a gold sheet with nine leaves and three large ivy leaves outlined in smooth wire and encircled by smooth and twisted wires. Though contemporary with single lion-head hoops (see Cat. no. 44), this type is apparently a western Mediterranean specialty.

Notes: Examples are known from Cumae, Taranto, and Capua (Higgins, *Greek and Roman Jewellery*, p. 163). An example at the Brooklyn Museum is from Ithaka (C. R. Williams, New York Historical Society, *Catalogue of Egyptian Antiquities: Gold and Silver Jewelry and Related Objects*, New York, 1924, pp. 149-50, nos. 86-87).

46

Hoop Earring: Bull's Head

Greek, second-first century B.C.
Height: 1⅜ in. (3.5 cm)
Publications: *Art Collection of Mrs. Henry Walters*, New York, Parke-Bernet Galleries, 1943, pp. 90-91 (ill.). Collection of Henry Walters before 1931; Mrs. Henry

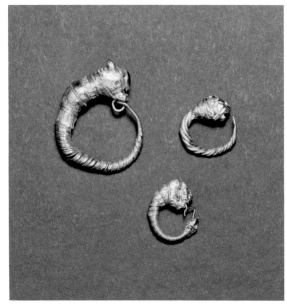

Cat. nos. 44, 45, 46

Walters, Sale, New York, Parke-Bernet Galleries, December 2, 1943, lot 522. (57.1730)

Two rounded strips and two pairs of twisted wire are wound together over a core to form a hoop that tapers at one end to form the ear wire. The elaborate collar of this gold earring, one of a pair, is formed of nine and a half long leaves edged with twisted wire, circles of smooth and twisted wire, and a hollow bead with twisted wire in the center held by rows of small leaves. The collar fits into a bull's head worked in repoussé. The hair is chased. The horns and ears are not made separately, and the eye was never inlaid. On the forehead is a drop-shaped garnet in a box setting edged by twisted wire. Around the setting at the nostrils is a garland made of four disks circled and partially connected by twisted wire. The loop at the bull's chin is twisted.

Notes: A similar earring from Egypt lacks the garnet on the forehead (Theodor Schreiber, *Die Alexandrinische Toreutic*, Leipzig, 1894, p. 305, fig. 29). Other bull-head hoops come from Egypt and Cyprus, again suggesting that this is an Eastern type (Higgins, *Greek and Roman Jewellery*, p. 162; and Georg Karo, "Die griechischrömischen Altertumer in Museum zu Kairo," *AA*, vol. 16, 1901, pp. 211-12, fig. 8). The addition of the garnet is typical of the later Hellenistic period, perhaps second-first century B.C.

47

Gold and Garnet Necklace

Greek, fourth-third century B.C.
Length overall: 19 5/16 in. (49.0 cm)
Length of finials: ¾ in. (1.9 cm)
Publications: *Jean Lambros et Giovanni Dattari collection*, Paris, 1912, p. 62.
Collection of Jean Lambros and Giovanni Dattari, Sale, Paris, Hôtel Drouot, June 17-19, 1912, no. 572.
(57.598)

This necklace is composed of eighty-five hollow gold beads, the openings of which are edged with twisted wire. The beads are threaded onto a chain made of double loops of wire constricted in their centers and twisted so that the end loops are in perpendicular planes. The bull-head finials have a collar consisting of a garnet bead held between gold cups that are encircled by smooth and twisted wire and a row of tongues. Each collar terminates in a gold cone and a ring of twisted wire and is attached to the chain by coiled hollow wire. The forelock and mane of each bull are chased. The inlay of the eyes is missing. One bull holds the hook in its mouth; the other, the loop.

Chain necklaces threaded with gold or garnet beads and ending in animal-head terminals were popular throughout the Hellenistic period. As with hoop earrings, lions' heads are the most popular terminals.

48

Hinged Gold Plaques

Greek, fourth-second century B.C.
Height: 2 11/16 in. (6.8 cm)
Width: 1⅝ in. (4.1 cm)
Publications: Randall, "Jewellery Through the Ages," p. 75; *The Dark Ages*, no. 120 (ill.).
Purchased from Leon Gruél, Paris, 1928. (57.1414)

These plaques, which may be part of the central ornament of a diadem, are composed of two sheets—one flat and one worked in repoussé—hinged together horizontally. On the rectangular plaque are two lyre volutes edged with twisted and smooth wires. Inside the volutes are palmettes and rosettes; outside are circles, ivy leaves, and rosettes. The rosettes and palmettes have petals and fronds made of gold leaf and

Cat. no. 47

Cat. no. 47

Cat. no. 48

are edged with twisted wire. The ivy leaves, circles, centers of the lyre volutes, and the large rosette were once inlaid. The seven small rosettes have granules at their centers. The upper sheet of the lower plaque is worked in repoussé to form the bust of a woman in high relief. Her hair is swept back beneath a diadem, and she is wearing a chiton and a himation. Her features are quite distinct and show evidence of chasing. On either side of the bust are a circle and an ivy leaf (once inlaid) and a rosette with a granule center. Both plaques are edged with a narrow gold strip and twisted and smooth wires. On the back traces of five loops remain. On one side of the rectangular plaque, there are two hinges.

Notes: The two plaques may be part of a diadem such as one from a tomb at Kyme (Aeolis) of the fourth-third century B.C. in London (*BMCJ*, no. 1632, pl. XXIX). Compare also a diadem in Berlin of the early second century B.C. (Greifenhagen, *Berlin I*, pl. 14).

49
Bracelet

Greek, fourth century B.C.
Maximum diameter of hoop: 2^{15}/16 in. (7.5 cm)
Length of finial: 1⅛ in. (2.9 cm)
Publications: Pierre Amandry, ''Orefèvrerie achéménide,'' *AK*, vol. 1, 1958, p. 15, n. 51, pl. 12, no. 34; Hoffmann and Davidson, *Greek Gold*, no. 57; *Antiquities and Primitive Art*, London, Christie, Manson & Woods, 1963, pp. 34-35, pl. 6; Dorothy Kent Hill,

Cat. no. 49 (see colorplate VII)

by David Stronach (sup., pp. 173-75). The Walters' bracelet is dated by him to the second half of the fourth century B.C. The bracelet and its mate were found in a group with an oval centerpiece from a diadem (Hoffmann and Davidson, *Greek Gold,* no. 5; sale catalogue, Christie, Manson & Woods, April 30, 1974, lot 170, pl. 9), a pair of bracelets with Herakles knots (Hoffmann and Davidson, *Greek Gold,* no. 54; sale catalogue, Christie, Manson & Woods, July 10, 1974, lot 235), a necklace with spearheads (sale catalogue, Christie, Manson & Woods, April 30, 1974, lot 171, pl. 9), two chains, a finger ring (Pierre Amandry, "A Review of Hoffmann and Davidson's *Greek Gold,*" *AJA,* vol. 71, p. 203), and a pair of earrings now in the Metropolitan Museum of Art (Andrew Oliver, Jr., "Greek, Roman and Etruscan Jewelry," *BMMA,* May 1966, p. 273, figs. 8-9; acc. no. 48.11.2-3).

Cat. no. 50   Cat. no. 50

"Greek Gold Bracelets," *BWAG,* vol. 26, no. 7, 1974; David Stronach, *Pasargadae,* Oxford, 1978, p. 174, nos. 10-11.

Probably from Western Asia Minor; offered to the Metropolitan Museum of Art in 1948 by H. von Aulock; later collection of Ake Wiberg (Apertin, Sweden); Sale, London, Christie, Manson & Woods, December 5, 1973, lots 140 and 141; said to have been found in Anatolia (Stronach, sup.). (57.2021)

The hoop of this bracelet, which is one of a pair, is formed of a wide tube of sheet gold folded into six flanges, twisted into a spiral, and bent round. Twisted wire is laid in the valleys and gathered at the ends of the hoop under the antelope-head finials, which are detachable. The antelopes' heads are made in two halves, worked in repoussé, and chased. The horns, made of thick twisted wire, are inserted separately. A strip of metal forms the collar of the finial and is decorated with three seven-frond palmettes, bordered above with a twisted and a smooth wire, below by a twisted wire between two smooth wires. A row of pointed leaves marks the transition from finial to hoop.

Notes: A pair of gold bracelets of spirally twisted wire with detachable antelope-head finials comes from the Pasargadae Treasure and belongs to the same series as this example. They are discussed as a group

50
Swivel Scarab Ring

Greek, fifth century B.C.
Diameter: $^{13}/_{16}$ in. (2.1 cm)
Length of scarab: $^{11}/_{16}$ in. (1.8 cm)
Publications: *The Morrison Collection,* London, Christie, Manson & Woods, 1898, p. 11; Burlington Fine Arts Club, *Exhibition of Ancient Greek Art,* London, 1904, p. 208, pl. 110, M 130; *Catalogue of the Collection of Engraved Gems... formed by Charles Newton-Robinson,* London, Christie, Manson & Woods, 1909, p. 6 (ill.).

Collection of Morrison, Sale, London, Christie, Manson & Woods, June 29, 1898, lot 58; collection of Charles Newton-Robinson, Sale, London, Christie, Manson & Woods, June 22, 1909, lot 7; purchased from Dikran Kelekian, 1909. (42.124)

The hollow gold hoop is triangular in section and has disk terminations. Wire is passed through the disks and the sard scarab and wound around the shoulders. The scarab is schematically modeled. Represented in intaglio is a crouching griffin on a simple ground line. There is no border.

Most archaic Greek gems were carved in the form of a scarab beetle. The type is ultimately of Egyptian origin and is thought to have passed to the Greeks via the Phoenicians probably on the island of Cyprus, which served as a crossroads for the eastern Mediterranean.

Notes: Comparable griffins are found on Greek and Greco-Persian gems of the fifth century B.C. (see Furtwängler, AG, pl. IX, no. 58, pl. XI, nos. 27, 41). The fact that the scarab is not meticulously modeled suggests that it is Greek rather than Etruscan. On the modeling of scarabs, see John Boardman, Archaic Greek Gems, London, 1968, pp. 13-15.

Cat. no. 51

51
Gold Ring

Greek, late fourth century B.C. (?)
Diameter: ⅞ in. (2.2 cm)
Length of bezel: 1¹/₁₆ in. (2.7 cm)
Collection of Henry Walters before 1931; Mrs. Henry Walters; purchased from Joseph Brummer, 1941. (57.1640)

The hoop of this ring is concave on the inside and convex on the outside. The pointed oval bezel is made of two flat sheets seamed together. The hoop and bezel are made separately.

This ring is of a standard type popular from the Late Archaic period. The typical Archaic form has a leaf-shaped bezel and a rounded hoop. Rings such as this example—with ovoid bezels and flat or concave hoops—are variations of the type.

Notes: John Boardman, Greek Gems and Finger Rings, London, 1970, pp. 212-14 (types I-IX).

52
Gold and Garnet Ring

Greek, third century B.C.
Diameter: ¹³/₁₆ in. (2.1 cm)
Height of bezel: 1⁵/₁₆ in. (3.3 cm)
Publications: The Morrison Collection, London, Christie, Manson & Woods, 1898, p. 32, pl. II; Furtwängler, AG, vol. 3, p. 167, fig. 117; Seymour de Ricci, Catalogue of a Collection of Ancient Rings formed by the late E. Guilhou, Paris, 1912, p. 40, no. 268, pl. V; Sir Arthur Evans, An Illustrated Selection of Greek and Greco-Roman Gems, Oxford, 1938, no. 76; Dorothy Kent Hill, "Some Hellenistic Carved Gems," JWAG, vol. 6, 1943, p. 66, figs. 2, 4; Marie-Louise Vollenweider, "Das Bildnis des Scipio Africanus," Museum Helveticum, Basel, from 1944, vol. 15, fasc. 1, 1958, p. 30, no. 32.
Collection of Morrison, Sale, London, Christie, Manson & Woods, 1898, lot 255, "said to be from Tarsus"; collection of E. Guilhou, 1912, purchased from Jacob Hirsch, 1942. (57.1699)

The broad hoop of this ring is rounded on the outside and flat on the inside. The shoulders are square. The oval bezel has a wide border and is set with a convex stone cut in intaglio with the head of Dionysos wearing an ivy wreath.

Notes: The ring is one of a group put together by Marie-Louise Vollenweider. She sees a resemblance in the portrait to Ptolemy IV Philopater (reigned 221-203 B.C.), who often was represented as Dionysos (see Vollenweider, sup.). Both Miss Vollenweider and Miss Hill date the ring to the third century B.C.

Cat. no. 52

The Olbia Treasure

In the spring of 1891, Russian peasants digging a plot of land near Olbia (a small town in the Crimea that was once an ancient Greek colony) came upon an ancient stone-faced tomb chamber in the midst of which were the remains of a bronze-footed wooden couch and the skeleton of a woman. The woman had been lavishly decked with jewelry: a wreath, gold and garnet earrings, two necklaces (one with a butterfly pendant), two gold rings, and a silver medallion of Aphrodite with two Erotes. A small gold coin to pay Charon to ferry her over the river Styx in the underworld had been placed in her mouth. Lying nearby were a multitude of gold ornaments, once probably sewn to her garments; a bronze mirror; a bone spoon; a clay lamp; and various pieces of pottery, including a lead-glazed terra cotta mug.

In 1894 this discovery was reported in a Russian publication that illustrated the butterfly necklace, the earrings, the lead-glazed mug, and other pottery and gold ornaments. A later Russian report, published in 1907, provided the additional information that the tomb had also contained a pair of silver cups, a silver ladle, a distaff, and a lead-glazed pitcher. The second report also described how the antiquities were dispersed: they were purchased from the peasants who found them by a local antiquities dealer who in turn sold them to a Moscow collector named Postnikov. Then, in a bizarre turn of events, archaeologists from St. Petersburg (Leningrad) to whom Postnikov showed his Olbia treasures cast such serious doubts on their

authenticity that, despite published arguments to the contrary, Postnikov decided to sell them.

Apprehensive of his ability to do so in Russia, he sold them (or at least some of them) to the London dealer Spink's. It was from Spink's that J. P. Morgan bought the silver cups, ladle, and distaff now in the Wadsworth Atheneum, Hartford, and the lead-glazed pitcher now in the Metropolitan Museum of Art. The lead-glazed mug never left Russia and is in the Pushkin Museum, Moscow. A British scholar, E. H. Minns, reported seeing the butterfly necklace for sale at Spink's in the early years of this century. No doubt it was sent to London by Postnikov with the silver from Olbia. The disposition of the rest of the jewelry and pottery is not known.

In the 1920s Henry Walters purchased the butterfly necklace, not from Spink's however, but from the Bachstitz Gallery of The Hague, acquiring it together with a group of gold ornaments all alleged to have been found at Olbia. This Olbia group, or Olbia Treasure as it has come to be known, belonged to a Frankfurt industrialist, F. L. von Gans, and was part of a large collection of ancient jewelry and other antiquities he began assembling after 1912, the year he had presented his first collection of antiquities to the Berlin Museum. In a folio catalogue of the second collection prepared for the Bachstitz Gallery in 1921, Robert Zahn, the assistant director of the Antiquities Department of the Berlin Museum, reported that Gans had obtained his Olbia pieces from another collector, Peter Mavrogordato, and that Mavrogordato had acquired the greater part of the group in the art market in 1913. And indeed a German archaeological report of 1913 illustrates much of the jewelry later published in the Bachstitz catalogue, describing it as having come from a tomb excavated not long before at Olbia. As confirmation of the provenance, the author of this report stated that he had re-excavated the tomb and had gleaned a gold ornament identical to ornaments alleged to have come from it. No mention was made of a tomb discovered in 1891, and none of the jewelry illustrated in the 1913 report is pictured in the earlier Russian accounts. Without consulting unpublished Russian archaeological sources, it seems impossible to determine whether the jewelry purchased by Mavrogordato in 1913 actually came from the tomb discovered in 1891 or from another burial in the same necropolis opened only a short time before 1913. Even Zahn recognized the problem in his comments in the 1921 Bachstitz catalogue: he considered the association likely but not incontrovertible.

The butterfly necklace that was the principal ornament of the 1891 tomb and is today the star of the Olbia Treasure must have been acquired directly from Spink's in London by Peter Mavrogordato, who was well acquainted with the circumstances of its discovery and surely recognized the object for what it was.

Representative of jewelry found in South Russian burials, the Olbia Treasure in the Walters Art Gallery is the blend of native and Greek styles one would expect to find in a region where generations of Greek colonists had lived side by side with local inhabitants who still retained their own non-Greek language and customs.

Andrew Oliver, Jr.

Cat. no. 53 (see colorplate VIII)

53

Necklace

Greek, first century B.C.
Length: 15 9/16 in. (39.5 cm)
Publications: Zahn, *Galerie Bachstitz*, pp. 29, 33,
pl. 26; Barbara Pfeiler Lippitz, ''Späthellenistische
Goldschmiedearbeiten,'' *AK* 15, 1972, p. 108, pl. 31.
Said to be from Olbia, South Russia. (57.385)

This gold necklace has a central blue oval stone (possibly a replacement) flanked by two green stones (one
missing), all three in box settings hinged and secured
with toggle pins. Below is a cruciform assemblage of
two garnets and two green stones, also in box settings
and hinged in the same manner. Chains to steady the

pendant run to the settings flanking the oval stone and
are secured by toggle pins ornamented with tiny rock
crystal beads. The rest of the necklace, comprising
pairs of green stones, garnets, and pearls, is ancient but
probably did not originally belong to the centerpiece of
mounted stones.

Notes: Robert Zahn, who first published this necklace, suggested that
the centerpiece was once hinged to the braided chains with dog-head
finials erroneously attached to a gold cosmetic jar in the Walters'
collection (acc. no. 57.380), and this seems likely. Such an arrangement would correspond not only to the design of the great butterfly
necklace (acc. no. 57.386), but also to that of a diadem in Athens from
Thessaly (*AK* 15, 1972, p. 108, pl. 30:1), another in Leningrad from
Artjukhov's barrow on the Taman peninsula, South Russia (Higgins,
Greek and Roman Jewellery, p. 169, fig. 27), and the center portion of
a necklace in the Cleveland Museum of Art (*Echoes from Olympus*,
Berkeley, 1974, no.192 [ill.]).

Cat. no. 54

lated and when shut can be secured by a pin that passes through intermeshing loops. All the members have a gold-sheet backing folded up at the side to hold the decorative elements in place. The centerpiece has a box setting for an oval stone or glass inlay (present stone is a modern replacement) surrounded by a floral design done in granules and wire, which includes oak and ivy leaves of green enamel. Slipped on the curved arms like sleeves are end pieces ornamented with three oval or circular stones in box settings. The sleeves adjacent to the centerpiece have oval garnets (?) flanked by green stones; the outer sleeves have round turquoise stones flanked by oval red ones. Many of the stones look like modern replacements. Elsewhere the arms are decorated with bands of cloisonné work: red, blue, and turquoise inlays in diamond, triangular, and round settings. In the center, overlapping leaves of granules and turquoise meet at a box setting. Flanking the leaves are troughs with pearls held in place by a wire running through loops. Major elements of the decoration are outlined with beading.

Notes: Hinged bracelets with toggle-pin clasps, commonplace in Roman and early Byzantine jewelry, originated in the late Hellenistic period. They were either flexible open hoops (Hoffmann and Davidson, *Greek Gold,* pp. 159 ff., no. 56 [ill.]) or centerpieces with curved, articulated arms, as shown here. Conceptually related to the Walters' bracelet is a bracelet in the National Museum, Athens, found in Thessaly (*AK* 15, 1972, pl. 33:2-3) and another from the collection of Lord Melchett, London, sold in the Basel art market in 1958 and said to have been found on the island of Mykonos (Münzen und Medaillen, Auktion XVIII, November 29, 1958, lot 155). But whereas the bracelets from Thessaly and Mykonos are in the mainstream of Greek jewelry, the Olbia bracelet is a hybrid of Greek and outlandish styles.

54

Bracelet

Greek, first century B.C.
Width: 2⅛ in. (5.4 cm)
Diameter: 2⅞ in. (7.3 cm)
Publications: Zahn, *Galerie Bachstitz,* pp. 27-28, 32-33, pl. 24; *The Dark Ages,* p. 33, no. 68 (ill.); C. R. Morey, "Art of the Dark Ages: A Unique Show," *The Art News,* February 20, 1937, p. 13 (ill.); Patricia Cowles, "Jewelry," *BWAG,* vol. 5, no. 4, January 1953 (2 ill.); Philippe Verdier, *Russian Art,* The Walters Art Gallery, 1959, no. 1 (ill.); Ross, *Migration Period,* p. 21; Randall, "Jewellery Through the Ages," p. 497, fig. 8; Barbara Pfeiler Lippitz, "Späthellenistische Goldschmiedearbeiten," *AK* 15, 1972, p. 117, pl. 31. Acquired by Peter Mavrogordato in the summer of 1913 with the story that it had come from a tomb discovered shortly before at Olbia; collection of F. L. von Gans; Robert Zahn was unable to confirm positively that it was found in the tomb opened at Olbia in 1891. (57.376)

This gold bracelet, one of a pair, consists of a centerpiece hinged to two curved arms. The arms are articu-

55

Earring

Greek, first century B.C.
Height: 2¼ in. (5.7 cm)
Publications: Zahn, *Galerie Bachstitz,* pp. 29-30, 33-34, pl. 25:D.
Said to be from Olbia, South Russia. (57.382)

This gold earring, one of a pair, has three flanged settings with brown stones (one missing), each set within a bead-edged frame, displayed against a roughly triangular sheet on the back of which the ear wire is attached. A pin concealed behind the transverse bar below the settings secures six pendant chains.

Crumpled caps at the ends of the chains once covered the tops of glass beads, which have long since disintegrated.

Notes: Two pairs of earrings in the Medieval Department of the Metropolitan Museum of Art, both said to be from Olbia, share the same scheme of design—stones mounted in a triangular arrangement with pendant chains below (acc. nos. 22.50.5-6, 22.50.7-8; sale catalogue, American Art Gallery, New York, Chmielowski collection, February 24, 1922, lots 692-93). The Walters' earring is also related to the earrings found with the butterfly necklace (*Drevnosti* 15:2, 1894, pp. 1 ff., pl. I:1) and to another pair from Kerch, South Russia (*Otchët*, 1903, p. 45, fig. 62).

Cat. no. 55

Cat. no. 56

56
Ring

Greek, first century B.C.
Diameter: $^{13}/_{16}$ in. (2.1 cm)
Publications: Zahn, *Galerie Bachstitz*, p. 30, pl. 26 F.
Said to be from Olbia, South Russia. (57.723)

This gold ring has an oval garnet set in the bezel and gently sloping shoulders.

Notes: A similar ring is in the British Museum (Higgins, *Greek and Roman Jewellery*, p. 175, pl. 53:F). Others have been found in Artjukhov's barrow on the Taman peninsula, South Russia; in Eretria, Greece (G. A. Papavasileos, *Peri ton en Euboia archaion taphon*, Athens, 1910, p. 57, pl. 14:14); Ancona, Italy (*NSc*, 1902, p. 460, fig. 29); and Delos, Greece (*BCH* 89, 1965, pl. 22:a; *BCH* 92, 1968, pp. 554-55). Their context suggests a date in the first century B.C.

57
Cosmetic Jar

Pontic, first century B.C.
Height overall: 4⅜ in. (11.1 cm)
Publications: Zahn, *Galerie Bachstitz*, pp. 30, 34, pl. 27:K.
Said to be from Olbia, South Russia. (57.381)

A cap fits snugly over the cylindrical neck of this gold jar. Two pairs of loops on the cap and jar are aligned to receive the suspension chains. Green stones keep the chains from slipping loose, and a horseshoe-shaped bar at the top is designed to fit comfortably over one's finger.

Cat. no. 57

Roman Jewelry

In his *Natural History* compiled in the seventh decade of the first century A.D., the encyclopedist Pliny attributed the origin of the Roman fashion for pearls and gems to the spoils of the victories of Pompey the Great in the East more than 130 years earlier. Pliny also drew attention to the taste among women for extravagant gold jewelry. Previously, Roman law had restricted its use: in the third century B.C. a woman could wear no more than half an ounce of gold, and only senators and knights were allowed gold rings. But gradually the rules were relaxed. The romanization of Etruria and the assumption by Rome of political power in the Mediterranean world—beginning with Magna Graecia (southern Italy and Sicily) in the late third century B.C. and Greece proper, Asia Minor, Syria, and Egypt in the second and first centuries B.C.—brought Italians into contact with countless new customs, among them jewelry.

Although the fashion and propriety of wearing jewelry developed through exposure to the East, Roman jewelry is a peculiar blend of the Eastern taste for colored stones with the Etruscan predilection for the use of flattened gold sheets to create abstractly contoured surfaces and volumes. Tertullian, a Christian writer flourishing about A.D. 200, remarked perceptively, yet sarcastically because he was condemning the practice of wearing jewelry in the first place, that stones and gold mutually enhanced one another (*On Female Dress*, VI). That is the essence of Roman jewelry. Of course, not all pieces exhibit this feature, but the tendency is evident in the earliest comprehensive view we have of Roman jewelry (contemporary with Pliny): namely, that based on the jewelry recovered from the ruins of houses at Pompeii and Herculaneum and such neighboring villas as the one at Boscoreale overwhelmed by the A.D. 79 eruption of Mount Vesuvius.

Well-to-do Romans had long vacationed in the Bay of Naples at the famous seaside resorts of Baia, Puteoli, Neapolis, and Herculaneum, and so we may assume that the jewelry found through modern excavation at the Vesuvian sites is representative of what was fashionable in the capital. But Roman jewelry was not limited to Rome and its environs, or even to Italy. We must also consider as Roman jewelry the products of the goldsmiths' guilds in Alexandria and Antioch and other cities where these craftsmen practiced their trade; the Roman jewelry widely exported and found today in all parts of the empire from Britain and the Spanish provinces in the West to Arabia Nabatea, Syria, and Cappadocia (central Asia Minor) in the East; and the jewelry made in the closing decades of the Roman Republic in the first century B.C. and in three and a half centuries of the Roman Empire proper, from the accession of Augustus as Emperor in 27 B.C. to the transfer of the capital to Constantinople in A.D. 330 by Constantine the Great shortly after his conversion to Christianity. During this period the emulation of Roman life by provincial cities of the empire had a homogenizing effect on the material culture of the Mediterranean world. Thus jewelry from one region is difficult to distinguish from that of another.

Burying jewelry with the deceased seems not to have been so common a custom as it was in earlier centuries. Nevertheless, numerous Roman tombs excavated in modern times have revealed sets of jewelry interred with the body: for a woman, earrings, bracelets, one or even two necklaces (occasionally with pendants), one or more rings, and frequently a wreath, perhaps worn only in death; in association with male burials, gold rings, often heavy ones. Much of the Roman jewelry in the Walters' collection must have originally come from such burials. Some pieces, however, are likely to be spoils from treasure troves. In times of peril, or for safekeeping, the family jewels might be secreted in a jar, perhaps even with a collection of gold or silver coins, for some reason never to be recovered by their original owner. One pair of earrings in the Walters' collection is reported to have come from the ruins of a house near Vesuvius (acc. no. 57.1914a, b).

Likenesses of women wearing jewelry of the very sort that has actually survived are seen in mosaics and wall paintings from Pompeii and Herculaneum and among funerary portraits from the Fayuum in Egypt. They serve to remind us that the earrings, necklaces, bracelets, and rings that follow were once personal possessions of real people worn next to the skin and treasured for a lifetime.

Andrew Oliver, Jr.

58

Earring

Roman, second century
Height: 1½ in. (3.8 cm)
Acquired before 1931. (57.1552)

A thick wire hoop, one end wound around the other for the clasp, forms the framework of this gold earring, which is one of a pair. The decoration is aligned in one plane around the outer edge of the hoop. At each side is a conical garnet in a flat-backed setting; at the bottom are three pearls hung from rings. Between the pearls and garnets are four rows of balls, six to a row, the center row concealing the fourth behind it. The balls and hoop are liberally sprinkled with granules on the front side only. Within the hoop is a disk with the face of Eros framed by twisted wire.

A disk, earwire, and pendant formed the basic Roman earring. The disk, or in many instances a mounted stone, concealed the S- or hooped-shaped earwire attached to its back side. The pendants were rigidly or flexibly secured to an extension of the earwire, the disk itself, or a transverse bar at the bottom of the disk.

Flattening his gold into thin sheets to gain maximum effect from the metal, the goldsmith built individual parts into composite geometric designs. Greek antecedents of this style can be seen in earrings in the form of disks with pendant amphorae, but in Roman jewelry recognizable shapes such as vases disappeared in favor of pure geometric ornament that emphasized the shimmering metal. Realistic renderings of human figures and animals, or their heads, do not occur except in certain "old fashion" pieces of the first century.

Mounted stones, especially garnets, green beryls, and pearls, become increasingly dominant components. In the midst of a commentary on pearl oysters, the Roman encyclopedist Pliny says, in an aside, that even the oyster's ability to close itself could not protect it from women's ears (*Natural History*, IX, 55, 111).

A rich series of earrings, generally dated to the second and third centuries, featured a cluster of small balls for the pendants, some resembling grapes and often dripping with granules. The different varieties must be indicative of regional styles, though these are difficult to identify today. Displaying a fan-like arrangement of ornament around the perimeter of a hollow hoop, the

Cat. no. 58

example shown here is a less common type of earring. With origins in Persian jewelry, the design had a subsequent history in Byzantine jewelry (see Cat. no. 110).

Notes: Although no exact parallels are known, this earring seems related to earrings excavated from a second-century Nabatean tomb at Mampsis in the Negev (*Archaeology* 24, 1971, 169 [ill.]). Others like the Mampsis pair are in the Rhode Island School of Design (Hackens, *Classical Jewelry*, pp. 113-15, nos. 50-51, nn. 1-3 [for further examples]).

59

Necklace and Pendant

Roman, the necklace first or early second century A.D., the pendant first century B.C. (?)
Length of necklace: 14½ in. (36.8 cm)
Diameter of pendant: 2¹¹/₁₆ in. (6.8 cm)
Acquired before 1931. (57.539)

The links of the chain of this gold necklace are double loops pinched and given a ninety-degree turn at the center. An openwork disk, fashioned as a wheel with twisted wire spokes and dotted with granules, forms part of the hook-and-eye clasp. The gold pendant, which originally may not have belonged with the necklace, shows in repoussé relief two Egyptian deities

Cat. no. 59

in Greco-Egyptian guise, both represented as sculptured busts on pedestals: Isis as Demeter, with a crescent emblem on her veil and carrying a torch; and Haroeris ("The Elder Horus"), as a falcon-headed man wearing the armor of a Roman legionary. The armor includes a breastplate sporting the face of Medusa.

Three types of necklace were predominant in the Roman period: (1) necklaces of multiple gold leaf ornaments linked together, (2) necklaces of colored stones, either pierced and threaded on gold links or set in mounts that were secured together, and (3) necklaces in the form of tightly braided or open loop chains with openwork wheels or more ambitious relief medallions as part of the hook-and-eye clasps. Threaded beads were sometimes introduced as isolated elements in necklaces of the first and third types (see Cat. no. 62).

Emerald beads, hexagonally faceted, were usually linked directly to one another (see Cat. no. 53). Garnets and other stones such as obsidian and carnelian, cut with fourteen sides (double cubes with beveled corners), were strung with sets of links or flattened links having a particular shape, such as a Knot of Herakles or a square knot (see Cat. no. 61). Beads of this distinctive cut were introduced as early as the first century B.C. and lasted until at least the mid-third century A.D.

Most pendants on chain necklaces were probably considered good luck charms, though of course pendant gold coins were a display of material wealth (see Cat. no. 63). The pendants ran free or were fastened to a link. Medallions with the head of Medusa boldly rendered in repoussé relief served as *apotropaic* (evil-averting) devices. A lady in a portrait from the Fayuum, now in the British Museum, seems to be wearing such a medallion.

Notes: A comparable necklace in the British Museum came from a second-century context at Backworth, England (*BMCJ*, no. 2738, p. 318, pl. LXI; Pfeiler, *Römischer Goldschmuck*, p. 71, pl. 19), while another in Athens, found at Eleutheropolis, Palestine, should date prior to A.D. 138 (*JIAN* 10, 1907, pl. VII:2). A comparable pendant showing Aphrodite on a goat was excavated in a late-second- or early-first-century B.C. context at Delos (*BCH* 89, 1965, pl. XXIII:c-d; *BCH* 92, 1968, pp. 557-64). The presence on the Walters' pendant of Isis and Haroeris, who were considered healers and saviors, suggests that the object was a good luck charm.

60

Necklace

Roman, second century
Length: 17 3/16 in. (43.7 cm)
Acquired before 1931. (57.1555)

This gold necklace has seventeen polygonal garnets graduated in size, each stone alternating with two figure-eight links. A disk forming part of the hook-and-eye clasp features a Medusa head in repoussé relief.

Cat. no. 60

61

Necklace

Roman, second century
Length: 15 in. (38.1 cm)
Acquired before 1931. (57.1549)

This gold necklace has eighteen flattened Knot of Herakles links alternating with hexagonal green stones and spherical blue beads, some of which are missing. A red sard stone set in a crimped gold setting shows in

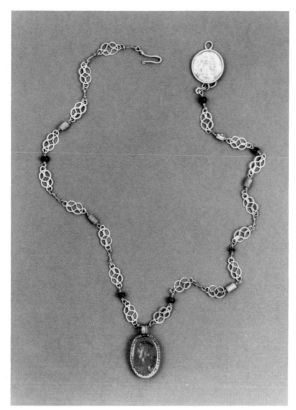

Cat. no. 61

groups with three green stone beads. An openwork disk punctuated with three hemispherical caps forms part of the hook-and-eye clasp.

Notes: Originally considered to be fifth- or sixth-century work, the necklace more likely dates from the second or third century. Beads interspersed among gold elements of necklaces have an early history in Roman jewelry. A necklace from Orbetello, Italy (dated to the first century only because of the superficial resemblance of its leaves to those on a necklace from Pompeii) has leaves grouped with green glass prismatic beads (*NSc*, 1958, p. 42, fig. 10). Nevertheless, isolated beads separated by short lengths of braided chain occur on necklaces from more firmly dated second- or third-century contexts, for example, one from near Tyre, Lebanon (*Bulletin du Musée de Beyrouth* 18, 89, F 401, pl. XIX [second or third century]) and others in the British Musuem from Beaurains, France (P. Bastien and C. Metzger, *Le trésor de Beaurains*, Wetteren, 1977, p. 165, pl. IV [late third century]).

63
Necklace with Pendant Coins

Roman, probably early third century
Length: 36 in. (91.4 cm)
Diameter of coins: 1$^{1}/_{16}$ in. (2.7 cm)
Publications: Zahn, *Schiller,* no. 111, pl. 61; Robert Zahn, "Die Sammlung Schiller," *Pantheon*, vol. 3, 1929, p. 130 (ill.); *The Mrs. Henry Walters Art Collection,* New York, Parke-Bernet, 1941, p. 420 (ill.); Christa Belting-Ihm, "Spätrömische Buckelarmringe mit Reliefdekor," *JRGZM* 10, 1963, p. 108, n. 44, pl. 18:1-2. Said to be from Egypt; collections of Adolph Schiller; Henry Walters before 1931; Mrs. Henry Walters, Sale, New York, Parke-Bernet Galleries, May 2, 1941, lot 1313. (57.1600)

This gold necklace is composed of four braided chains that are gathered together, passed through two large beads, and crossed over to the opposite bead, where the ends are secured. The ends of the chains are fitted through holes crudely punched into the sides of the beads and are fastened by buttons inside. The overlapping chains give the impression that part of the necklace has eight chains. The length of the necklace can be adjusted by sliding the chains through the beads, thereby altering the amount of overlap. Bringing the beads together lengthens the necklace; moving them apart shortens it. The beads are faceted and ornamented with rosettes, palmettes, and scallop shells. Collars keep the open ends from fraying.

Seven *aurei* (gold coins) are mounted in frames with cut-out borders. An eighth pendant, second from the

intaglio the bust of a youth. The gold disk shows Eros leaning on an arrow near Aphrodite, who crouches as she does in the statue by the Greek sculptor Doidalsos. Neither the sard nor the disk need have originally belonged to the necklace.

Notes: Flattened Knot of Herakles links occur on another necklace in the Walters' collection (acc. no. 57.1556) and on a necklace in the British Museum from Tortosa, Syria (*BMCJ*, p. 316, no. 2730, pl. LX).

62
Necklace

Roman, second or third century
Length: 14½ in. (36.8 cm)
Publications: *Byzantine Art,* no. 427, pl. LVIII.
Acquired before 1931. (57.524)

Gold leaves edged with flattened wire and dotted with clusters of granules are graduated in size and linked in

Cat. no. 62

right, is actually a pair of disks, or bracteates, set back-to-back to resemble a gold coin. Seven tubular spacers separate the pendants. From left to right, the coins show the portraits of Vespasian, Nerva, Domitian, the Elder Faustina, Marciana, Vitellius, and (skipping the disk with busts of Luna and Sol) Vespasian again.

As Cornelius C. Vermeule has shown, the practice of mounting coins became increasingly common in the third century (''Numismatics in Antiquity,'' *Swiss Numismatic Review* 54, 1975, pp. 5-32). Inflation under the Severan emperors during this period and the resulting lighter weight of new coins caused the intrinsic value of the earlier and heavier *aurei* of the first and second centuries to rise above their face value. Older *aurei* were prudently withdrawn from circulation and hoarded as bullion. For this reason and also because of their historic significance, they were occasionally mounted for display in jewelry as medals.

On this example the coins range from Vitellius, A.D. 69, to the Elder Faustina, wife of Antonius Pius, deified after her death in A.D. 140-41. Hers is the least worn.

Notes: A similar necklace in the Metropolitan Museum of Art, with five coins ranging in date from A.D. 168 to 227, is said to have been found at Memphis, Egypt (acc. no. 36.9.1; Cornelius C. Vermeule, ''Numismatics in Antiquity,'' *Swiss Numismatic Review* 54, 1975, pp. 16-18, no. 26 [ill.], nos. 2-3). Another with four coins, ranging from about A.D. 140 to 238, is in the Kunsthistorische Museum, Vienna (Robert Forrer, *Reallexikon*, 1907, p. 518, pl. 134:1). Yet another, with similar quadruple chains, a pair of beads, and spacers, but without pendant coins, was found in association with third-century unmounted coins in the Hadra cemetery, Alexandria, giving credence to the alleged Egyptian provenances of the Walters' and Metropolitan Museum's necklaces (E. Breccia, in *Le Musée Gréco Romain*, 1925-31, 29, pl. XXI, fig. 78). A quadruple chain, two beads, and spacer without mounted coins is in a private collection in Germany (*Antiken aus Rheinischem Privatbesitz*, Bonn, 1973, p. 257, no. 414, pl. 185). Three mounted coins of the Valerians, senior and junior of the years A.D. 254-56, and two beads but no chains found at Rabakovacsi, Hungary, are in the National Museum, Budapest (E. B. Thomas, *Studien zur Geschichte und Philosopie des Altertums* [ed. J. Harmatta], Budapest, 1968, pp. 343-46, figs. 7, 9).

Cat. no. 63 (see colorplate IX)

Cat. no. 64

64

Pendant

Roman, fourth century
Diameter: 3 11/16 in. (9.4 cm)
Publications: S. P. Noe, "Bibliography of Greek Coin Hoards," *Numismatic Notes and Monographs,* no. 78, New York, 1937, p. 14, no. 6; M. C. Ross, "Notes on Byzantine Gold and Silversmith's Work," *JWAG,* vol. 18, 1955, pp. 63-65, fig. 9.
Purchased from Dikran Kelekian, 1928. (57.526)

The upper border and attachment that once secured this gold pendant to a necklace are missing. A diademed portrait of Alexander the Great framed by two beaded moldings is shown in repoussé relief. Surrounding the portrait is a wreath border made by punching through the gold sheet with a sharp tool. The edge is rolled back and crimped to form beading. Around his ear Alexander wears the ram's horn of Ammon. This Egyptian god, who was equated by the Greeks with Zeus, had a cult and oracle at the Siwa oasis in eastern Libya. Alexander visited the oasis, and some ancient writers say he was even deified by the oracle, thus accounting for the many portraits showing him with the ram's horn attribute.

Notes: The pendant recalls three pendants now divided between the Louvre and the Dumbarton Oaks Collection, Washington, D.C., each with a gold coin of about A.D. 320-30 and an openwork wreath border (Sale, London, Christie, Manson & Woods, October 19, 1970, among lots 197-200; Cornelius C. Vermeule, *Swiss Numismatic Revue* 54, 1975, pp. 27-28 [ill. 9]). Similar openwork occurs on a pair of fourth-century bracelets divided between the St. Louis Art Museum and the Berlin Museum (Greifenhagen, *Berlin I,* fig. 62, pl. 55:7) and on another bracelet of this date in the British Museum (*BMCJ,* no. 2817, pl. LXV).

65

Bracelet

Roman, first century
Inside diameter: 2 9/16 in. (6.5 cm)
Outside diameter: 3 1/4 in. (8.2 cm)
Acquired before 1931. (57.528)

This gold bracelet is in the form of a serpent. The head and tail are modeled in a lifelike manner, with skin indicated by crosshatching, but the rest of the hoop is left plain. Leaf-shaped ornament and clusters of dots mark the termination of the crosshatching.

Serpent bracelets made of a solid hoop are one of two kinds of Roman bracelets developed from versions used earlier in the Greek world. The type was frequently seen on Roman funerary portraits from the Fayuum and perhaps was originally a Ptolemaic specialty. The other type, a hinged strap bracelet, is exemplified by the bracelet from Olbia (Cat. no. 54). Instead of being made of a solid bar, hoops were also fashioned from hollow tubes spirally wound together

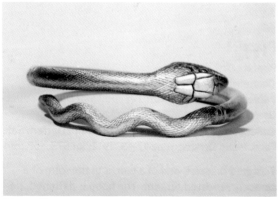

Cat. no. 65

and capped at each end with sepents' or lions' heads. On some examples a mounted stone is displayed between the heads; on others the mounted stone stands alone without head finials. A Roman mosaic from Antioch shows a servant girl bringing a pair of such bracelets on a tray to her mistress (*AJA,* vol. 42, 1938, p. 213, fig. 8). Other varieties of Roman bracelets include those fashioned from simple chains, gold links, or mounted stones linked together.

Notes: Pairs of similar bracelets have been found at Pompeii (Breglia, *Napoli,* nos. 831-32, pl. 36:6, II) and at Boscoreale near Pompeii (Foundation Piot, Monuments et Mémoires 5, 1899, pp. 265-67, no. 110-11, fig. 57); other examples are in the British Museum (Higgins, *Greek and Roman Jewellery,* p. 187, pl. 61:E), the collection of Norbert Schimmel (O. M. Muscarella, ed., *Ancient Art, The Norbert Schimmel Collection,* 1974, no. 71 [ill.]), and the Benaki Museum, Athens (Berta Segall, *Museum Benaki Athen, Katalog der Goldshmiedearbeiten,* 1938, pp. 115 ff., nos. 171-74, pl. 37-38).

Cat. no. 66

66
Bracelet

Roman, first century
Diameter: 2¾ in. (7.0 cm)
Publications: *Jean Lambros et Giovanni Dattari collection,* Paris, 1912, p. 62.
Collection of Jean Lambros and Giovanni Dattari, Sale, Paris, Hôtel Drouot, June 17-19, 1912, lot 573. (57.534)

This gold bracelet, one of a pair, is in the form of a cursorily rendered serpent. The hoop is flattened, depriving the reptile of the lifelike appearance of the

previous example. In imitation of the natural appearance of a serpent's body, skin is indicated on the outer angled surface of the bracelet by crosshatching and on the inner chamfered edges by chevrons.

Notes: Bracelets of this flattened design were also made with a serpent's head at each end (Zahn, *Schiller,* p. 87, pls. 48-49; Münzen und Medaillen, Auktion XVIII, November 29, 1958, lot 160).

67
Ring

Roman, first century
Outside diameter: 1 in. (2.5 cm)
Height: 1⅛ in. (2.9 cm)
Purchased from Michel Abemayor, 1930. (57. 1538)

This gold ring has a serpent's head at each end of the hoop. The heads are turned back against their necks. The skin and details of the heads are crudely indicated by short strokes and crosshatching.

Rings were worn by both men and women on any finger except the middle, although the fourth finger of the left hand was the most favored. They served a variety of functions: some had a practical use as signets (seals with which individuals could mark letters and documents such as wills with their own distinctive devices); others were a mark of dignity or rank, a custom

Cat. no. 67

apparently adopted from the Etruscans. For women rings might be a token of betrothal. Rings could also be purely ornamental and were often collected for the gems they displayed.

Such an extensive variety of rings has come down to us from the Roman world that it is difficult to mention more than a few basic kinds. Like serpent bracelets, serpent rings such as the one shown here are a legacy of the Greek world to early Roman taste. Signet rings with a stone cut in intaglio and set into the bezel continued from Greek versions without abrupt changes in style. Sometimes the device was cut directly into the gold bezel of the ring (see Cat. no.68).

Hoops were substantial or slender. They could be round in section, but more often the outer face was round or angled, and the inner face was flat. In many rings of the third century, the lower part of the hoop was distinguished and set off from the broad shouldering of the upper part. Rings were surely worn more constantly than other jewelry. Commenting on the natural wear of material things, the first-century B.C. Latin poet and philosopher Lucretius observed that as the years go by the ring on the finger becomes thin beneath by wearing (*De Rerum Natura*, I, 312).

68
Ring

Roman, third century
Maximum diameter: ⅝ in. (1.6 cm)
Purchased from Dikran Kelekian, 1911. (57.1020)

This gold ring has an elliptical hoop that broadens at the shoulders and a flat-topped oval bezel. Within an engraved circle on the bezel is an intaglio showing the figure of Eros—with one leg on a rock— holding a ball. A length of wire is coiled on the hoop.

69
Ring

Roman, first or second century
Diameter: ⁹/₁₆ in. (1.4 cm)
Purchased from John Khayat, New York, 1956.
(57.1863)

The dotted Greek inscription on this child's gold ring reads ΑΥΞΑΝΕ (grow).

Notes: A gold ring with an inscribed bezel of similar shape came from a late-first-century tomb near Tyre, Lebanon (*Bulletin du Musée de Beyrouth* 18, 81, F 426, pl. XVIII). Others are in Berlin (Greifenhagen, *Berlin II*, p. 83, pl. 61:12-13) and the Metropolitan Museum of Art (Gisela M. A. Richter, *Catalogue of Engraved Gems, Greek, Etruscan and Roman*, 1956, p. 120, no. 598, pl. LXV).

70
Wedding Ring

Roman, third or fourth century
Diameter: ⅝ in. (1.6 cm)
Length of bezel: 1⅛ in. (2.9 cm)
Publications: *Catalogue vente à Rome, Alessandro Castellani Collection*, March 17-April 10, 1884, p. 120 (ill.); *CIL*, 13, 3, 1901, 631, no. 10024, 63 (the inscription); S. de Ricci, *Catalogue of a Collection of Ancient Rings formed by the late E. Guilhou*, Paris, 1912, p. 58, no. 439, pl. VII; *Catalogue of the Superb Collection of Rings formed by the late Monsieur E. Guilhou*, London, Sotheby & Co., November 9, 1937, pl. XIV; *Byzan-*

Cat. no. 68

Cat. no. 69

Cat. no. 70

tine Art, no. 501; *The Notable Art Collection . . . of the late Joseph Brummer,* New York, Parke-Bernet, May 12, 1949, p. 58 (ill.).
Said to have been found in France; collections of Alessandro Castellani, Sale, Rome, March 17-April 10, 1884, lot 924; E. Guilhou, Sale, London, Sotheby & Co., November 9, 1937, lot 406; Joseph Brummer, Sale, New York, Parke-Bernet Galleries, May 12, 1949, lot 254; purchased 1949. (57.1824)

The hoop of this ring is a flat hexagonal gold band ornamented with openwork. On the back is a Latin inscription reading DVLCIS VIVAS (Live Sweetly). The bezel is elongated in a fingernail-like projection, giving an indication of where it might have been worn. Two blue-and-white cameo stones are inlaid in raised settings, an oval one on the overhang with a splendid representation of a ship and an almond-shaped one with a Greek inscription reading EYTYXI (Good Luck).

Notes: Rings of similar design with wedding inscriptions are in the Musée d'Art et d'Histoire, Brussels, and the Rothschild collection, Paris (*Archaeologia Aeliana,* 4th ser., 26, 1948, pp. 139-42, pl. V:2-3). A simpler wedding band is in the Corbridge Museum, England (ibid., 13, 1936, pp. 310-19, pl. XXV).

Migration Jewelry

The hordes of Asian horsemen that overran the Roman Empire were originally a mixture of agricultural and nomadic herding tribes. Their way of life necessitated carrying their wealth with them and wearing it as a badge of rank, and jewelry became a practical means of doing so. The ultimate explosion of migrations in the fourth century caused the agrarian peoples to imitate their herding neighbors, and for a period of centuries, jewelry became the bullion, the badge of office, and the normal ornament of the Huns, the Goths, the Vandals, and the many other tribes of central and western Asia who, having been gradually forced from their lands, migrated towards the fertile areas of Europe.

The descent of the Huns from central Asia in the fourth century was the major event that compelled the tribes north of the Black Sea, in western Russia, and in eastern Europe to begin a series of migratory wars that were to continue until the tenth century. The pressure of tribe against tribe caused the ultimate breakdown of the frontiers of the Roman Empire. It also led to the development of a complex history of tribal alliances, warfare, and treachery.

The earlier systems of political checks and balances of the Romans both in the East and West had kept the Germans out of Gaul and the Asian tribes in relatively settled areas beyond the limits of the Eastern Empire. Trade with Roman colonies north of the Black Sea brought the nomadic horsemen into contact with Greco-Roman jewelry traditions and allowed them to set up standard trade routes with India to acquire gar-

nets, almandines, and other precious stones to create their ornaments. By the time of the attacks of the Huns, major tribes such as the Avars, Goths, Alans, Sarmatians, Burgundians, and Lombards had all established traditions of ornament and jewelry. It decorated their horses and themselves in daily life and was carefully buried with them in their graves.

Our modern knowledge of these great tribal migrations is based in part on the great sagas and epic poems of oral literature but depends more solidly on the excavations of thousands of graves across Europe. Traces of a powerful tribe like the Visigoths may be followed from South Russia into Rumania and Greece, over into Italy, down the west coast and up the eastern one, across southern France, where the tribe remained for the larger part of a century, and finally into Spain, where they settled. With this great migration went the traditions carried from the original homeland, many of which were altered to some extent by time and artistic development and by the acceptance of allies and other cultures along the route.

Barbarian style included several different elements, which stemmed from far-flung sources. Of major importance was the "animal style" of central Asia, which had some relation with Persian and Near Eastern traditions. A rich source of techniques came from the Greco-Roman world, as Greek craftsmen had begun producing rich gold jewelry north of the Black Sea as early as the fourth century B.C. Such techniques as chip carving, filigree, granulation, and inlay with precious stones and glass pastes were well known. They were adopted rather differently by the various tribes, and many were abstracted and turned into linear patterns. Color was particularly favored by many barbarians, and a polychrome style, quite different from that of Greece and Rome, was developed, employing the use of inlays, stones, glass pastes, and enamel.

The simplicity of Hunnish work contrasts sharply with the jewelry of the Franks, where abstracted birds, geometric designs, interlace, animals' heads, glass inlays, and Christian griffins drinking from the Fountain of Life show a myriad of influences. The materials changed as new territories were conquered. The round Frankish fibulae from the Rhineland were of gold and filigree, while the great buckles from the Frankish graveyard at Tabariane in Aquitaine were plated with tin engraved with interlace.

Particularly spectacular and varied is the Hunnish jewelry found at various sites from Russia to Hungary and lower Austria. Examples of fourth-century style include four pieces lavishly decorated with almandines and garnets, which probably formed the ornaments of an important warrior (see Cat. no. 73): a chamfron studded with 102 jewels for the horse; a handle for the warrior's whip, with both gems and granulation; and two strips of harness ornament decorated *en suite.* Early fifth-century style is represented by the armlet for the upper arm decorated with a large garnet (Cat. no. 75), which relates to others found in Russia. Another Hunnish find, which has parallels to those from northern Austria, is all of silver.

The Langobards of northern Italy settled in lands rich with tradition. These lands neighbored powerful Byzantine strongholds, and it is hardly surprising that their jewelry reflects these civilizing influences and that their earrings, for instance, are close imitations of Byzantine style.

The Franks were the first of the tribes to be Christianized. Their king, Clovis, was baptized in A.D. 498, and various other tribes joined either the Aryan or the Catholic church. The cross, therefore, begins to appear as an ornament in Frankish jewelry, and the drinking griffin of the pierced belt buckle (Cat. no. 85) is paralleled on early Christian altar frontals from Italy and Byzantium. On some Burgundian buckles, there is a representation of a head with a cross above it, representing the Holy Face.

Other symbols, such as the eagle, which was common to both Frankish and Visigothic jewelry, undoubtedly had mythic significance. Among the most striking examples of the polychrome style are a pair of Visigothic eagle fibulae (one of which is shown here), found in Spain, which are subdivided into compartments filled with green and blue glass pastes, garnets, mother-of-pearl (?), and small cabochon crystals (Cat. no. 89). Worn as a pair with pendant stones from their tails, they must have made a noble effect.

Square-headed brooches were introduced into England by the invasions of the Angles and Saxons. Nearly identical types can be found on the continent, but there is an interesting progression of changes that takes place in the jewelry forms in England as old forms degenerated or were elaborated or altered. The new waves of tribal immigrants, as recorded by the Venerable Bede, helped to keep fresh the connections with continental patterns.

The last phases of European migratory activity are connected with the Vikings. Their jewelry included torques and rings of twisted wire, which descend in concept from the earliest Celtic jewelry of the Middle Bronze Age. The heavy silver torque to be worn around the upper arm (Cat. no. 95), though Viking in origin, was appropriately found in Ireland, where its warrior owner was buried.

Richard H. Randall, Jr.

71

Ribbon Armlet

Scottish, Middle Bronze Age, ca. 1000 B.C.
Diameter: 4 in. (10.2 cm)
Publications: Philippe Verdier, "Gold from Ancient Ireland," *BWAG*, vol. 6, no. 7, April 1954, (called Irish);
John M. Coles "The 1857 Law Farm Hoard," *The Antiquaries Journal*, vol. 48, pt. II, pp. 169 ff., pl. 46, nos. 26, 27.

Collection of Sir William Gordon Cumming; purchased New York, 1953. (57.1847)

This torque for the upper arm is made of a ribbon of sheet gold twisted in an even corkscrew pattern and joined with a hook-and-eye clasp. Excavated in Morayshire in 1857, it stands at the beginning of a Celtic jewelry tradition that continued in Scotland and Ireland into the eighth century and as late as the tenth century with the Vikings.

Cat. no. 71

Cat. no. 72

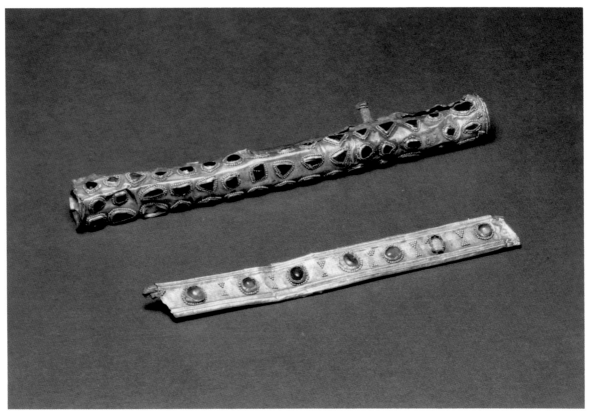

Cat. no. 73 (see colorplate X)

72

Torque

Celtic, fourth-second century B.C.
Diameter: 4¹⁵/₁₆ in. (12.5 cm)
Found in the Scheldt River; collection of Hugo Olse; gift of Mrs. Carol L. Brewster, 1973. (54.2502)

This bronze torque for the neck is engraved with La Tène designs on either side of the opening and with striations on the flattened terminals, which expand abruptly. The torque was broken in half in ancient times.

73

Jeweled Garniture

Hunnish, fourth century
Length of whip handle: 5¾ in. (14.6 cm)
Length of mount: 4¹⁵/₁₆ in. (12.5 cm)

Publications: *Byzantine Art,* no. 841; Richard Winston, ''The Barbarians,'' *Horizon,* vol. 12, no. 3, 1970, p. 73 (colorplate).
Purchased from Arnold Seligman, Rey and Co., 1929. (57.1050, 57.1052)

Set with carnelians and other stones in granulated settings, these two ornaments of sheet gold, together with two other pieces found with them but not shown here, represent the trappings of an important Hunnish horseman. The cylindrical tube served as the handle of a whip. Its ends, one of which is closed, are decorated with twisted gold wires and triangles of granulation. A bronze rivet affixes the tube to the shaft. The strip of gold, probably either a harness or scabbard mount, is set with a single row of carnelians and has a border turned over copper. The stones are divided by double triangles of granulation. The strip is broken and bent at the ends.

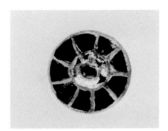

Cat. no. 74

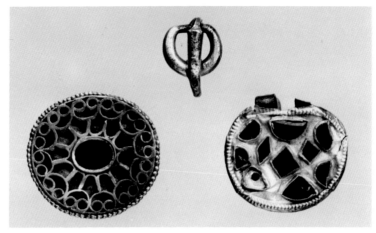

Cat. no. 74

74

Two Fibulae, a Buckle Plate, and a Buckle

Hunnish (probably South Russia) fourth-fifth century
Length of buckle: ¾ in. (1.9 cm)
Length of buckle plate: 1¼ in. (3.2 cm)
Diameter of wheel fibula: ¾ in. (1.9 cm)
Width of oval fibula: 1½ in. (3.8 cm)
Publications: Ross, *Migration Period*, p. 36.
Acquired 1929. (57.557A, 57.557B, 57.556, 57.558)

Presumably found together, this group comprises a gold buckle, a gold buckle plate backed with bronze and set with odd-shaped pieces of carnelian, a gold wheel fibula set with garnets and a central carnelian, and an oval fibula of openwork in gold, originally set with carnelian, of which only the central inlay remains.

75

Armlet

Hunnish (probably South Russia) early fifth century
Diameter: 4½ in. (11.4 cm)
Publications: Ross, *Migration Period*, pp. 38, 40.
Acquired from Daguerre, Paris, 1928. (57.1082)

This tubular gold armlet has a cinquefoil clasp composed of four hemispheres decorated with granulation and a central domical garnet. The reverse side is decorated with twisted gold wire, and the attaching collars and surfaces between the spheres are granulated. The pin is a modern replacement.

Cat. no. 75

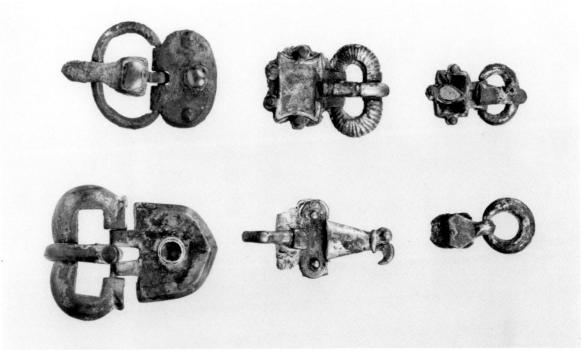

Cat. no. 76

76

Buckles

Hunnish (probably Russia) early fifth century
Lengths: (a) 2⅛ in. (5.4 cm), (b) 1¼ in. (3.2 cm),
(c) 1⅜ in. (3.5 cm), (d) 1¾ in. (4.5 cm),
(e) 1⅛ in. (2.9 cm), (f) 2¼ in. (5.7 cm)
Publications: Ross, *Migration Period*, p. 44.
Acquired from Arthur Sambon, Paris, 1930. (57.658,
54.1918, 57.659, 57.656, 53.24, 57.657)

This group includes (a) a silver buckle set with pastes,
(b) a bronze-gilt buckle lacking its tongue, (c) a
bronze-gilt buckle, its plate framed with four rivets, (d)
a silver buckle plate with a bird-head finial, (e) a bronze
buckle with two red paste inlays, and (f) a silver buckle
set with a single garnet.

77

Ten Graduated Polyhedral Beads

Ostragothic, fifth century
Width: ¼ to ⅜ in. (.6 to 1.0 cm)

Collection of Joseph Chmielowski, Sale, American Art
Gallery, February 23-25, 1922, lot 710; Henry Walters;
Mrs. Henry Walters, Sale, December 1-4, 1943; lot
537; purchased from the Hammer Galleries, 1945.
(57.1746)

These gold polyhedral beads set with garnets probably
formed part of a necklace. Found at Olbia, the beads
are similar to many earrings of the period found in
South Russia.

Cat. no. 77

Cat. no. 78

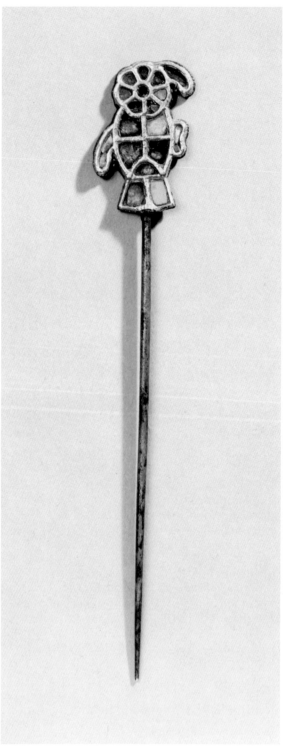

78
Gold Plated Bronze Ring

Frankish, sixth century
Diameter: 1¼ in. (3.2 cm)
Publications: Ross, *Migration Period,* p.60.
Collection of Henry Walters; Mrs. Henry Walters;
acquired from Joseph Brummer, 1941. (57.1679)

The bezel of this ring is formed of stepped squares. The
upper face is incised with a sunburst in imitation of an
intaglio setting. The hoop, which is broken, develops a
strong median ridge as it approaches the bezel.

79
Pin with Bird Terminal

Frankish, late sixth century
Length: 6½ in. (16.5 cm)
Publications: Ross, *Migration Period,* p. 62.
Acquired from the Carlebach Gallery, 1959. (57.1883)

This plain silver pin terminates in a stylized bird, which
is overlaid with gold foil and divided into compart-
ments set with thin garnets over crosshatched gold foil.
Similar pieces have been found in France near Arras
(Champagne) and at Herpes (Charente) and are in the
Museum fur Vor-und-Frugeschichte, Berlin.

Cat. no. 79

80

Digitated Fibula

Frankish, second half of sixth century
Length: 3½ in. (8.9 cm)
Publications: Ross, *Migration Period,* p. 60.
Acquired 1959. (54.2444)

Five knobs inset with red glass pastes radiate from this bronze-gilt plate, which has incised geometric patterns. The bow is bordered with inscribed spirals and set with three garnets. The stem is a restoration.

81

Bow Fibula

Frankish (probably Lorraine), ca. 600 A.D.
Length: 4⅛ in. (10.5 cm)
Publications: Ross, *Migration Period,* p. 68.
Acquired from the Carlebach Gallery, 1959. (54.2445)

The fields of this bronze fibula are carved with interlace ornament and bordered with flat strips inlaid with zig-zag borders in niello. The plate has an undulating border, and the fibula terminates in a stylized animal's head. There are traces of gilding over the whole piece.

Cat. nos. 80, 81

82

Circular Fibula

Frankish, ca. 600 A.D.
Diameter: 1⅝ in. (4.1 cm)
Publications: Ross, *Migration Period,* p. 68.
Acquired from the Carlebach Gallery, 1959. (57.1884)

The bronze body of this fibula is overlaid with a sheet of
silver decorated in repoussé and set with red pastes and
a central domical green paste bead. The design is of a
Maltese cross with palmettes between the arms. The
iron pin is missing.

83

Animal Fibula

Frankish, seventh century
Length: 1⅜ in. (3.5 cm)
Publications: Ross, *Migration Period,* p. 70; C.
Boulanger, ''Le Cimetière Mérovingien de Monceau,''
Bulletin Archéologique, 1908, pp. 328 ff., pl. 29, no. 4.
Purchased by Henry Walters before 1931. (57.571)

The bronze base-plate is faced with sheet gold attached by gold rivets. The animal's body is decorated
with filigree of twisted wire, and the eye is set with a
red glass paste. A pair of related fibulae were found in
France at Monceau (Oise).

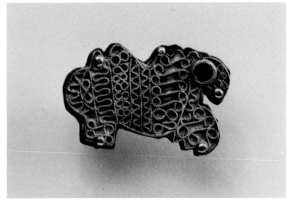

Cat. no. 83

Cat. no. 84

Cat. no. 82

84

Round Fibula

Frankish (probably Rhineland), seventh century
Diameter: 1¾ in. (4.5 cm)
Publications: Ross, *Migration Period,* p. 72.
Gift of H. Kevorkian, 1947. (57.1714)

The gold face of this fibula is inlaid in a bronze disk,
decorated with filigree, and set with eight glass pastes
in red, blue, and green around a larger central blue
paste.

Cat. no. 85

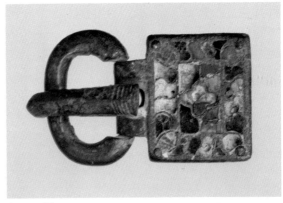

Cat. no. 86

85

Bronze Buckle with a Griffin

Frankish, seventh century
Length: 4 in. (10.2 cm)
Publications: Herbert Kühn, ''Die Germanischen
Greifenschnallen der Völkerwanderungzeit,'' *Ipek*,
1934, pp. 77 ff., no. 30. *Byzantine Art*, no. 859; Ross,
Migration Period, p. 76; *Romans and Barbarians*, no.
175.
Collections of Victor Gay; Joseph Brummer, Sale, New
York, May 12, 1949, lot 278. (54.2343)

This buckle is broken, and part of its loop is missing.
The bronze plate is pierced with a griffin drinking from
a fountain. The surface is treated with linear designs
and punched circles. The buckle relates to one found in
Picardy, though the majority of the type have been
found in Burgundy and Switzerland.

86

Buckle and Plate

Frankish, seventh century
Length: 2¾ in. (7.0 cm)
Publications: *Byzantine Art*, no. 851; Ross, *Migration
Period*, p. 80.
Acquired by Henry Walters from Daguerre, Paris, 1930.
(54.424)

The tongue of this bronze buckle is decorated with
incised lines. The square plate is divided into cloisons
set with garnets and blue stones, some of which are
missing.

87

Gold and Paste Earring

Langobard, seventh century
Height: 2 in. (5.1 cm)
Acquired from Joseph Brummer, New York, 1927.
(57.475)

The front of this earring is decorated with a cross in
green pastes, with four gold bosses between the arms.
The back is a gold hemisphere with filigree decoration,
and there is a ring at the bottom for a pendant. The
hoop is circular.

Cat. no. 87

88

Small Gold Ring

Langobard, seventh century
Diameter: ⅝ in. (1.6 cm)
Publications: Ross, *Migration Period*, p. 96.
Collections of Henry Walters before 1931; Mrs. Henry Walters; acquired from Joseph Brummer, New York, 1941. (57.1604)

This ring, probably made for a child, is set with two pearls and an emerald. A zigzag wire between two larger plain wires forms the hoop.

Cat. no. 88

89

Eagle Fibula

Visigothic, second half of sixth century
Length: 5⅝ in. (14.3 cm)
Publications: O. von Falke, "Zur Wiedereröffnung der Walters Art Gallery in Baltimore," *Pantheon*, vol. 18, 1936, p. 346; J. Martinez Santa-Olalla, "Westgotische Adlerfibeln aus Spanien," *Germania*, vol. 10, 1936, pp. 47 ff.; G. Thiry, *Die Vogelfibeln, Rheinische Forschungen zur Vorgeschichte* 3, Bonn, 1939, no. 16, pl. 16; H. Kühn, "Die Grossen Adlerfibeln der Völkerwanderungzeit," *Ipek*, 1939-40, p. 134, pl. 58; Ramón Menéndez Pidal (ed.), *Historia de España* 3, España Visigoda, Madrid, 1940, p. 122, fig. 45; J. Martinez Santa-Olalla, "Nuevas Fibulas Aquiliformes Hispanovisigodas," *Archivo Español Archeologia*, vol. 14, 1940-41, p. 36; H. Schlunk, "Arte Visigodo," *Ars*

Hispaniae 2, Madrid, 1947, p. 309, fig. 326; W. Holmquist, *Germanic Art,* Stockholm, 1955, pl. 15; Ross, *Migration Period,* p. 100.
Purchased by Henry Walters from Daguerre, Paris, 1930. (54.421)

This large and well-preserved fibula, one of a reversed pair, was found at Tierra de Barros (Badajoz) and is noted for its fluid lines, which contrast with the majority of eagle fibulae from Spain (see Cat. no. 90). Made of a bronze core, it is overlaid with sheet gold and inlaid with blue and green pastes and garnets. The raised boss in the center is inset with a cabochon crystal, and the eye of the bird is inset with an amethyst set in a circle of mother-of-pearl (?). The brow is inset with a blue paste (now largely missing). Many of the pastes in the body are fractured. Originally, the eagle had attachments at the tail for three pendants. The pin is missing.

90

Eagle Fibula

Visigothic, sixth or early seventh century
Length: 4¼ in. (10.8 cm)
Publications: J. Martinez Santa-Olalla, "Sobre Algunos Hallazgos de Bronces Visigóticos en España," *Ipek*, 1931, pp. 58 ff., fig. 1; H. Zeiss, *Die Grabfunde aus dem Spanischen Westgotenreich*, Berlin, 1934, pp. 19, 104, 194, pl. 6, no. 3; G. Thiry, *Die Vogelfibeln, Rheinische Forschungen zur Vorgeschichte* 3, Bonn, 1939, p. 68, pl. 4, no. 22 (erroneously attributes Walters Art Gallery example to Museo Nacionale, Madrid); J. Martinez Santa-Olalla, "Nuevas Fibulas Aquiliformes Hispanovisigodas," *Archivo Español Archeologia*, vol. 14, 1940-41, pl. 3, fig. 7; H. Kühn, "Die Grossen Adlerfibeln der Völkerwanderungszeit," *Ipek*, 1939-40, pp. 136 ff., and esp. p. 136, pl. 59 (7); *L'Art Mérovingien* (exhibition catalogue), Brussels, 1954, p. 43, pl. 27; two more examples formerly in the von Diergardt collection and now in the Römisch-Germanisches Museum, Cologne; Ross, *Migration Period,* p. 102.
Collection of Meto (?); purchased by Henry Walters from Seligman, Paris, 1910. (54.423)

This is a typical example of the Visigothic eagle brooch. In this case it is made of bronze and divided into small cloisons inset with garnets, blue stones, and mother-

Cat. no. 89 (see colorplate XI)

Cat. no. 90

Art, New York, 1954, no. 2; Randall, ''Jewellery Through the Ages,'' p. 496, fig. 6b.
Purchased from Daguerre, Paris, October 10, 1930. (57.560)

Said to have been found in Estramadura, this large earring, one of a pair, is formed of seven stones and pearls mounted in gold collars, with stamped foliate designs in thin gold on the back of each setting. It has a large hoop with one ball finial for suspension and three amethyst pendants, each with a green glass bead on the gold wire.

Notes: The workmanship was called Byzantine by Marvin Ross but is nearly identical in treatment to the Crown of Recesvinto, the votive crown, and a pair of earrings of Visigothic workmanship in the Archaeological Museum, Madrid.

Cat. no. 91

of-pearl (?). There is a central shield-like boss, and the eye was a large inlay. Many of the stones are missing, as is the pin. It was found in Spain at Herrera de Pisuerga (Palencia).

91
Earring
Visigothic, sixth century
Height: 4⁷/₁₆ in. (11.3 cm)
Width: 1¹¹/₁₆ in. (4.3 cm)
Publications: *Byzantine Art,* no. 854; The Metropolitan Museum of Art, The Cloisters, *Spanish Medieval*

92

Silver Pin

Irish, sixth-eighth century
Length: 4 in. (10.2 cm)
Publications: Ross, *Migration Period,* p. 110.
Collections of Robert Day of Cork, Sale, London, Sotheby, May 19-22, 1913, lot 458; William Randolph Hearst; Joseph Brummer, Sale, New York, May 12, 1949, lot 276. (57.1832)

Found in a County Galway crannog, this unusually elegant pin has a double-knob head and a spiral line around the pin for decoration.

93

Bronze Pin

Irish, sixth-eighth century
Length: 9 in. (22.9 cm)
Publications: Ross, *Migration Period,* p. 112.
Collections of Robert Day of Cork, Sale, London, Sotheby, May 19-22, 1913, lot 355; William Randolph Hearst; Joseph Brummer, Sale, New York, May 12, 1949, lot 276. (54.2340)

An interesting form is displayed in this elegantly tapering pin with two collars and a finial curved back in a spiral. It was found at Armagh in 1886.

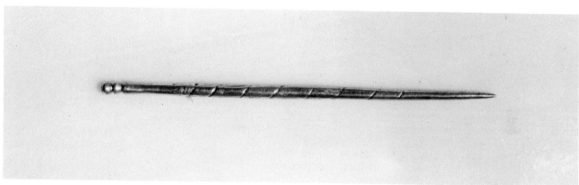

Cat. no. 92

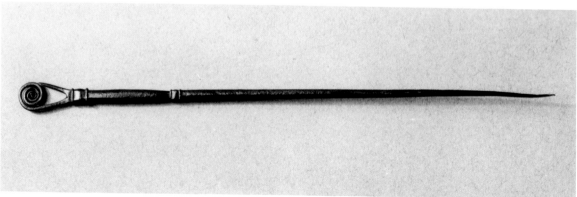

Cat. no. 93

94

Bronze Penannular Brooch

Irish, sixth-seventh century
Length: 5 in. (12.7 cm)
Publications: H. E. Kilbride-Jones, ''The Evolution of
the Penannular Brooches with Zoomorphic Terminals in
Great Britain and Ireland,'' *Proceedings of the Royal
Irish Academy*, vol. 43, 1935-37, pp. 379 ff.; Ross,
Migration Period, p. 114; Randall, ''Jewellery Through
the Ages,'' p. 497, fig. 7.

Cat. no. 94

Cat. no. 95

Collections of Robert Day of Cork; William Randolph Hearst collection; Joseph Brummer, Sale, New York, May 12, 1949, lot 277. (54.2341)

The bronze ring of this brooch is hatched to imitate wire binding for half its circumference and for the other half is flattened and carved with scrolling plant ornament. The head of the pin is decorated with three deeply cut ovals, and the pin is incised with linear ornament on its faceted central section. Worn on the left shoulder, such brooches developed from Roman models but were greatly elaborated in Ireland.

95

Silver Armlet

Viking, seventh-eighth century
Diameter: 4¾ in. (12.1 cm)
Publications: Ross, *Migration Period*, p. 116.
Collections of Robert Day of Cork, Sale, London, Sotheby, May 19-22, 1913, lot 452, and pl. XIX; William Randolph Hearst collection; gift of members of the Board of Trustees, 1941. (57.1599)

This massive armlet of thick, twisted silver strands was found at Fenit, County Kerry, Ireland.

96

Silver Ring

Viking, sixth-eighth century
Diameter: 1 in. (2.5 cm)
Publications: Ross, *Migration Period*, p. 118.
Collection of Alastair Bradley Martin; gift of Ralph M. Chait, 1954. (57.1850)

Cat. no. 96

Composed of two strands of thick silver wire twisted together to form a single strand, this type of ring was called "ring money." This example is said to have been found in Ireland along with other specimens.

Cat. no. 97

97

Bronze Box Brooch

Viking, eleventh century
Diameter: 2⅜ in. (6.0 cm)
Publications: Ross, *Migration Period*, p. 118.
Purchased from James Graham, New York, 1952. (54.2373)

This cast bronze brooch with a basketry design is a typical Viking pattern and was found at Böda on the Swedish island of Öland. The pin is missing, and several areas of the background are broken through the front surface. In the center is an ornament of superimposed squares with a highly polished central circle.

Byzantine Jewelry

No empire was ever richer in its jewelry traditions than that of the Byzantines. As the heirs of the territories and peoples of the Eastern Roman Empire (founded after the Emperor Constantine moved the capital to Constantinople in A.D. 330), the Byzantines inherited Greece, Egypt, the entire Near East, parts of Russian Asia, and the littoral of North Africa, along with the highly developed skills of the craftsmen in these great lands.

Within the Byzantine Empire there were two major stylistic approaches: one, established when Greece dominated the Mediterranean, which was classical and realistic, and another, which came ultimately from Persia and the East via the trade routes, which was abstract. Neither style ever completely dominated the arts of the Byzantines; rather they existed side by side or co-mingled in various new forms.

The jewelry of the empire reflects both styles. For instance, cameos and coins remain for the most part in the Hellenistic tradition, but many other pieces, such as the gold belt buckle (Cat. no. 104), follow a patterned and abstract Eastern tradition. Among the new developments in Constantinople was cloisonné enameling—with hieratic figures in brilliant colors floated on a gold ground—recalling the great art of mosaic, which was brought to its height in the decoration of the palaces and churches of Byzantium.

One of the important monuments for the study of the imperial use of jewelry is San Vitale in Ravenna with its famous mosaics completed in A.D. 547, which show a procession led by the Emperor Justinian and his Empress Theodora. The empress is dressed in a rich textile woven of gold threads and studded with pearls and gems. On her head is a crown of gold, enamel, and stones; around her neck, a series of pearl, enamel, and gem necklaces; and on her ears, earrings with long drops of pearls. Justinian wears a diadem and a large brooch with triple pendants, the special insignia of the emperor. This jeweled splendor became part of the ritual of the Byzantine court and was duly imitated not only by the courtiers, but in all the capitals and dependencies of the empire.

Cloisonné enamel was often used in Byzantine jewelry for pendants of saints or for tiny religious medallions on earrings, where the chief decoration was gold filigree. Sickle-shaped earrings of filigree, with projecting triangles of filigree and pearls, became a frequent ornament of ladies of the empire, though the Alexandrians seem to have favored long drops of several pearls. In necklaces the effects of color and glitter were achieved by the use of myriad colored stones alternating with pierced golden disks and clasps.

Among the rings from this period is a fine gold marriage ring of distinguished simplicity with the symbolic clasped hands (Cat. no. 101). A late signet ring bears engraved heraldic lions and religious inscriptions but is set with a gem of classical origin showing the figure of Pan (Cat. no. 103).

The Byzantine Empire controlled the lands of the eastern Mediterranean in political fact, but within its varying and immense borders it fostered many cultures and artistic styles. In the Balkans one finds a strong leaning toward the animal style in bracelets with silver reliefs. Some combine repoussé and niello decoration, such as the silver earring with a pair of entwined birds (Cat. no. 113), which is identical to one found in Hungary. Other regions, like South Russia, imitate the fine technique of cloisonné enameling. For example, the crescent-shaped earring from Kiev (Cat. no. 112) relates in shape and form to the silver one from the Balkans but is of gold decorated with a pair of birds in cloisonné enamel.

Even after the fall of Constantinople in 1453, the influence of Byzantine style continued unabated in corners of the empire such as Greece, the Balkans, South Russia, and isolated monasteries like Mount Sinai. One of the richest examples of Byzantine work is the reliquary pendant of the Metropolitan Arsenius of Serres (Cat. no. 114), which was probably produced on the island of Chalke in the sixteenth century. The case of the reliquary is decorated on the back and inside with elegant niello decoration and lavish inscriptions. The interior is shaped to contain four relics and a small finely made gold and niello reliquary cross with pearl decoration, which is somewhat earlier in date. Set with cabochon jewels on a ground of filigree, the front of the pendant has as a centerpiece an amethyst cameo of the Virgin and Child. The cosmopolitan tradition of this pendant combines Eastern Christian iconography,

Greek goldsmithing, pagan gem settings, and the most current of European niello design. Like many earlier examples, it shows the polygot traditions of the great Eastern Empire—traditions that continued long after the empire's demise.

The Byzantine tradition was carried west into Europe by the crusaders and, periodically, from the time of Charlemagne onwards, by other means such as trade and intermarriage. For example, the Princess Theophano, daughter of the Byzantine Emperor Romanus II, married the German Emperor Otto II in A.D. 972 and brought with her as a dowry marvelous creations from the Byzantine Empire. Textiles and other products were received through trade and affected the styles of Carolingian France, Ottonian Germany, and the Italian peninsula. Few actual remnants of this exchange exist, but there are vessels of imperial quality in the treasures of San Marco in Venice and the royal French collection, now in the Cabinet de Medailles in Paris. Two such vessels are also in America: the serpentine bowl of Suger's chalice for St. Denis in the National Gallery of Art and the agate Rubens Vase in the Walters Art Gallery, which is decorated in the late Roman tradition with satyrs and vine leaves. Of jewelry there is all too little evidence, as gems and enamels tended to be reset, and the goldsmith's work was sent to the crucible.

Richard H. Randall, Jr.

Cat. no. 98

98
Fibula

Byzantine, fifth century
Length: 4¹/₁₆ in. (10.3 cm)
Width: 2⅜ in. (6.0 cm)
Publications: H. J. H. van Buchem, "Bemerkungen zu den Dreiknopffibeln des vierten Jahrhunderts," *Bulletin Antieke Beschaving,* Jaargang, vol. 48, 1973, pp. 143-57.
Purchased at Gimbel Brothers, 1941; gift of Marvin C. Ross, 1941. (54.2263)

This bronze crossbow fibula of the three-knobbed type is cast with a formal pattern on the stem and has striations on the bow. The head is pierced with two holes that flank the central knob. The pin is missing. The type is well known from find sites in Pannonia (Hungary).

99
Diadem

Byzantine, fifth century
Length: 12¼ in. (31.1 cm)
Width: 1 in. (2.5 cm)
Publications: *Byzantine Art,* no. 419; Deér, "Mittelalterliche Frauenkronen," p. 447, fig. 49g.
Collection of Gilhou, Sale, Paris, July 16-18, 1905, lot 272, pl. X. (57.549)

This diadem is formed of ten thin gold rectangular panels pierced with basket and foliate patterns. The two end panels have rounded corners. Each panel was originally set with five stones or pearls, but only the central amethysts, which alternate with green feldspar, have survived. The panels are pierced with holes for sewing to a headband of either cloth or leather.

Notes: Deér and others have accepted the theory that this is a diadem

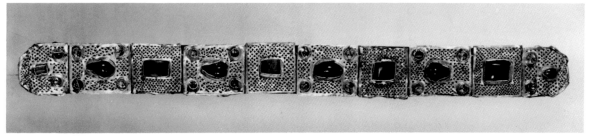

Cat. no. 99

and have illustrated similar pieces in use. Etienne Coche de la Ferté in *Bijoux du Haut Moyen Age* (Lausanne [Payot], 1962, pl. IV) rejects the evidence and interprets this piece and two others as jeweled collars rather than diadems.

100
Bracelet

Byzantine, fifth-seventh century
Diameter: 3 in. (7.6 cm)
Purchased 1951. (57.1844)

This bracelet is made of tubular gold that swells to a ridge on one side. On the opposite side is a simulated fastener of five embossed ribs.

Notes: This example is part of a group of three bracelets, two of which are now in the Royal Ontario Musuem, considered to have been Mycenaean (*BMCJ*, pl. VIII, nos. 800, 801). More recently the attribution was altered to Byzantine on the basis of bracelets from the Treasure of Mersine. (cf. Nikodim P. Kondakov, "Trésors Russes (et Byzantins) Enfouis," *Russkie Klady*, vol. 1, 1896; and André Grabar, "Un Médaillon en or provenant de Mersine en Cilicie," *Dumbarton Oaks Papers*, vol. 6, fig. 2, no. 10).

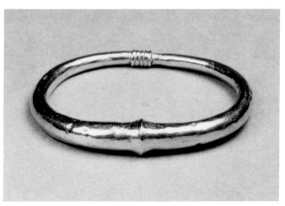

Cat. no. 100

101
Marriage Ring

Byzantine, sixth century
Diameter of hoop: ¾ in. (1.9 cm)
Diameter of bezel: ⅝ in. (1.6 cm)
Publications: *Byzantine Art*, no. 508, pl. 65; The University of Notre Dame, *The Arts of Christian Antiquity*, Notre Dame, 1957, no. 26.
Gift of Mrs. Saidie A. May, November 6, 1942.
(57.1715)

This ring is cast in gold with a wide convex band with beaded borders. The circular bezel shows clasped hands in relief within two circles of beading.

Cat. no. 101

102
Ring

Byzantine, sixth-seventh century
Diameter of hoop: ¹³/₁₆ in. (2.1 cm)
Diameter of bezel: ⅝ in. (1.6 cm)
Publications: *Byzantine Art*, no. 509.
Acquired by Henry Walters (?) before 1931. (57.1582)

This gold ring has a plain hoop and a high bezel treated with a row of fleur-de-lys in high relief. The bezel is inset with a disk nielloed with a cross within a wreath.

Cat. no. 102

Cat. no. 102

103
Signet Ring

Byzantine, twelfth century
Diameter: 1 1/16 in. (2.7 cm)
Length of bezel: 1/2 in. (1.3 cm)
Publications: *Byzantine Art,* no. 518, pl. 65.
Purchased by Henry Walters before 1931. (57.1580)

This gold hoop is deeply incised with ornament, and on the shoulders are rampant lions within pointed ovals. The collar is inscribed with the words of the Twenty-sixth Psalm, "Lord, my light and my saviour, whom shall I fear?" The Roman nicolo (?) intaglio depicts Pan.

Cat. no. 103

104
Buckle

Byzantine, seventh century
Length: 2 3/8 in. (6.0 cm)
Width: 13/16 in. (2.1 cm)
Publications: Herbert Kühn, "Wictige Langobardische Funde in Amerikanischen Sammlungen," *Ipek, vol. 12, 1938, p. 179, pl. 59, fig. 5; Byzantine Art,* no. 469, pl. 66; Cooper Union Museum, *Enamel,* New York, 1954, no. 15.
Acquired by Henry Walters (?) before 1931. (57.1891)

The round and lyre-shaped sunken areas of this small gold buckle with beaded edges are pierced with geometric designs that reveal an underlayer of white meerschaum.

Cat. no. 104

105
Pectoral Cross

Byzantine, tenth-eleventh century
Height: 2 3/16 in. (5.6 cm)
Width: 1 7/16 in. (3.7 cm)
Publications: *Byzantine Art,* no. 442; Charles Diehl, *Byzantium: Greatness and Decline,* New Brunswick, N. J., 1957, p. 227.
Purchased by Henry Walters from Leon Gruél, Paris, 1928. (44. 153)

Each arm of this hollow cross of sheet gold has a rounded end emphasized with three bosses and a pierced cross. The central medallion has a roped border, within which is a standing figure of Christ on one

Cat. no. 105

side and a bust of Christ on the other, carried out in blue, red, and green cloisonné enamel. The surfaces of the cross are slightly crushed, and the lower arm is bent.

106

Necklace

Byzantine fifth-sixth century
Length: 16⅜ in. (41.6 cm)
Publications: *Byzantine Art,* no. 429.
Acquired by Henry Walters (?) before 1931. (57.544)

This necklace of alternating stones and small pearls strung on gold wire includes nine pink quartz beads, three glass beads, and thirteen pearls. The clasp is formed of two circular openwork disks with Greek crosses and leaves.

Cat. nos. 106, 108

Cat. no. 107 (one of a pair)

107

Pair of Earrings

Byzantine (probably Egypt), fourth-fifth century
Height: 2½ in. (6.4 cm)
Publications: Marvin C. Ross, ''A Byzantine Treasure in Detroit,'' *The Art Quarterly,* vol. 22, no. 3, Autumn 1959, p. 231, figs. 5, 7.
Purchased from Sheik Ismael, Cairo, 1930. (57.594-95)

These earrings are simple loops with single pendants made of gold spacers and three small baroque pearls.

108

Earring

Byzantine, sixth century
Height: 3¾ in. (9.5 cm)
Publications: *Byzantine Art,* no. 479.
Collection of Khawam (?); purchased from Dikran Kelekian; Mrs. Henry Walters, Sale, New York, Parke-Bernet, December 2, 1943, lot 519; purchased 1943. (57.1729)

This hoop earring has three pendant plaited chains,

each terminating in a hollow gold cross and pendant amethyst. The crosses have striated surfaces and a central cell, which was originally filled with a green vitreous paste (now largely missing).

109

Pair of Earrings

Early Byzantine, sixth century
Height of each: 1 in. (2.5 cm)
Acquired by Henry Walters (?) before 1931. (57.606-7)

The outer edge of the hollow gold hoop is lined with granules. A convex shield, dotted in the center, is situated at one end of the hoop; a rigid ring ornament is attached to the bottom. The hoop and granules of each earring are completely worn through on one side, exposing their interiors.

Notes: Similar earrings have been found in Sicily together with coins of the Emperor Tiberius II (reigned A.D. 578-82) (*Byzantinische Zeitschrift* 19, 1910, p. 464, no. 3, pl. II:1, p. 474, fig. 16). Related earrings are in Berlin (Greifenhagen, *Berlin II,* 65, pl. 51:11) and the Dumbarton Oaks Collection, Washington, D.C. (Ross, Dumbarton Oaks II, 1965, 66, no. 85, pl. 48).

Cat. no. 109

110

Pair of Earrings

Byzantine, sixth century
Height: 2 in. (5.1 cm)
Publications: *Byzantine Art,* no. 478a, pl. 64.
Purchased from Dikran Kelekian, Paris, December 16, 1926. (57.1574-75)

From a central gold semicircle decorated with filigree spring five radial bars. Decorated with filigree borders and granulation, the bars expand slightly and terminate in openwork filigree patterns.

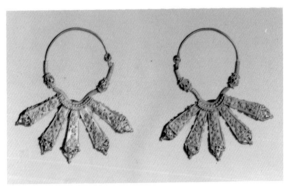

Cat. no. 110

111

Gold Earring

South Russian, eleventh century
Height: 2⅛ in. (5.4 cm)
Publications: *Byzantine Art,* no. 485 (as Langobard, seventh century).
Joseph Brummer, Sale, New York, May 12, 1949, lot 253. (57.1823)

Three openwork balls of filigree separated by two circles of filigree decorate this large loop. The plain half of the loop is hinged and secured with a pin.

112

Earring

Russian (Kiev), eleventh-twelfth century
Height overall: 2⅛ in. (5.4 cm)
Width: 1¹⁵⁄₁₆ in. (4.9 cm)
Acquired by Henry Walters (?) before 1931. (44.297)

Cat. no. 111

This large gold *kolt* (crescent-shaped earring) is formed of two shaped disks with a simple loop at the top for the ear. The front is decorated with addorsed birds divided by a small spade-shaped tree in cloisonné enamel of red, green, blue, and off-white. The back is divided into small geometric areas of enamel.

Cat. no. 112 (see colorplate XII)

113

Earring

Byzantine (the Balkans ?), twelfth century
Height: 1 9/16 in. (4.0 cm)
Width: 1¾ in.(4.4 cm)
Publications: *Byzantine Art,* no. 490; Ross and Downey, ''An Emperor's Gift,'' pp. 22 ff., fig. 5.
Said to have been found in Constantinople; purchased from Joseph Brummer, 1920s. (57.1073)

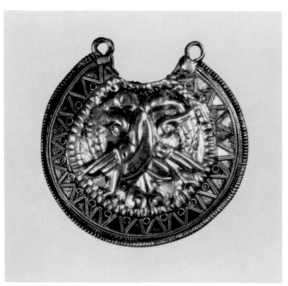

Cat. no. 113

This silver crescent-shaped earring is embossed on the front with an intertwined pair of gilded birds within a beaded circle. The outer borders of applied wire include a band of triangular and circular ornaments, two loops of twisted wire, and an outer beaded border. The ear loop was attached to paired rings at the top, one of which is missing. The back is embossed with the identical design and is deeply dented.

Notes: A nearly identical earring is in the National Museum, Budapest, without a history. Ross surmised that these were either made in Constantinople or inspired by Constantinopolitan work.

114

Reliquary Pendant and Cross

Byzantine (Greece), sixteenth century
Height overall: 3⅛ in. (7.9 cm)
Width overall: 2 13/16 in. (7.1 cm)
Height of cross: 2 1/16 in. (5.2 cm)
Publications: *Byzantine Art,* no. 448; Marvin C. Ross and Basil Laourdas, ''The Pendant Jewel of the Metropolitan Arsenius,'' *Essays in Honor of Georg Swarzenski,* Chicago, 1952, pp. 181-84.
Purchased by Henry Walters before 1931. (57.1511 a,b,c)

This jewel is formed of a hinged reliquary case with compartments for six relics and a small pectoral cross. The front of the gold pendant has a large amethyst

Cat. no. 114 (see colorplate XIII)

cameo of the Virgin and Child set within a border of cabochon emeralds, rubies, and pearls against a ground of filigree. The back is decorated with similar filigree set with a large green stone in the center, a circle of six cabochon rubies, and an outer circle of green stones, rubies, and pearls. The outer edge of the pendant has a border of fifteen pearls in filigree settings. The hinge is broken.

The inner face of the back-plate of the reliquary is decorated in niello with a floral pattern surrounding the compartments for the relics. The small gold cross from the reliquary has a figure of Christ in niello on a hatched ground with inscriptions. There are two pearls on either side of the suspension loop.

The inscription may be translated, "Arsenius, the most holy metropolitan of Serres and hypertimos (and) substituting for (the metropolitan of) Cesaria-Capadocia, God be helper." There are three other conventional religious inscriptions in Greek. On the edges of the pectoral cross is a second inscription to the same Arsenius: "Dedicated by the most holy Metropolitan of Serres, Arsenius, to the monastery of the Holy Trinity called Esoptron on the Island of Chalke." The Metropolitan Arsenius, who is known from three other inscriptions, was Metropolitan of Serres in the mid-sixteenth century.

115

Bronze Pectoral Cross

Byzantine (possibly Syria), sixth-seventh century
Height: 2 1/16 in. (5.2 cm)
Joseph Brummer, Sale, New York, May 12, 1949, lot 288. (54.2352)

The figure of the standing Christ with a cross above his head is on the front of this small pectoral cast in bronze. Inscriptions, now worn, are in each arm of the cross. The cross was hinged at the top. The back is missing.

Cat. no. 115

116

Bronze Pectoral Cross

Byzantine, eleventh century
Height: 4¾ in. (12.1 cm)
Purchased from A La Viella Russie, New York, 1949.
(54. 2367)

The front of this cross is engraved in a highly stylized manner with the praying Virgin and the Christ Child between angels. On the back is a medallion bust of a saint. The cross is hinged on the suspension ring to reveal a cavity for a relic and is secured at the base by a tripartite latch.

Cat. no. 116

Medieval Jewelry

In the late Middle Ages, from the twelfth to the fifteenth century, jewelry was worn sparingly by both men and women. Medieval costume was relatively simple, often of heavy wool, and a brooch or clasp at the neck was the chief ornament of the period. In addition there were occasional belt buckles of precious and gilded metal and a large variety of finger rings of silver and gold.

The materials were carefully selected, as every precious stone was seen in light of its special properties and amuletic value. Many stones were thought to have certain protective significance, such as the sapphire so often used in bishops' rings. According to the lapidary tradition, the sapphire made its wearer beloved of God and man, in addition to protecting him from injury, fraud, and terror. The green toadstone, which was thought to be found in the forehead of the toad, was believed to cure dropsy, and the amethyst, to prevent drunkenness.

More exotic materials like unicorn's horn, coral, and ancient flint arrowheads (called "serpents' tongues") were suspended around the neck or used in jewels for their prophylactic value. Each of these materials was thought to be useful in detecting poison, but some had other traits as well. Coral was a general protection against disease and was sometimes related to strengthening the heart. Its use as an amulet around the necks of children probably led to the habit of using it for teething in the Renaissance and later. An early depiction of it may be seen around the neck of the Christ Child in the *Madonna and Child* by Barnaba da Modena, dated 1367, in the Staedel Institute, Frankfurt.

In addition to the materials themselves, there was great faith in the protective quality of inscriptions, particularly religious ones. Many brooches and rings bear the name of Jesus, the INRI inscription from the Crucifixion, or Gabriel's salutation, Ave Maria. The names of the three kings—Caspar, Balthasar, and Melchior—were used to protect travelers and also as a protection against epilepsy. The 1380 inventory of King Charles V reveals that he owned a brooch with their names. The name of a patron saint was also often employed as a protective inscription.

The literature of the fourteenth and fifteenth centuries indicates that many magical words were recommended for engraving upon rings or jewelry—among them, words that identified constellations and zodiacal signs and words employed to prevent specific diseases. As a charm against falling sickness, the word *Ananazpata* was used; and against toothache, the words *BURO Berto Berneto*. The word *AGLA*, usually interpreted as standing for *Atha Gebri Leilan Adonai* (Thou art might for ever, oh Lord), is thought to have had amuletic importance.

Certain medieval jewels were symbols or badges of office. Every bishop received a ring at his consecration, a tradition related to the use of papal rings as signs of authority. Messengers and marriage brokers wore emblems of their office, as can be seen on the figure in the background of the *Merode Altarpiece* by the Master of Flemalle, at the Cloisters. In an account of 1420, the Duke of Burgundy pays a goldsmith for twenty silver badges of the arms of Burgundy to be worn by the knights and officers of his household.

Often made of lesser materials like lead, many of these badges have been recovered from the River Seine and are now in the collections of such institutions as the Cluny Museum and the Walters Art Gallery. Some indicate political affiliations and were worn as hat badges or attached to the costume. Others are signs of pilgrimages and indicate that the wearer had traveled to Santiago de Compostela or some other great religious shrine. The custom of wearing such pilgrim badges is recorded as early as 1183 in the Chronicles of Saint Denis, where the badge of Our Lady of Puy is carefully described.

Necklaces were rather uncommon until the fifteenth century, as indicated both by representations and by inventories. An unusual example in gold and enamel formed "like the leaves and branches of May" is recorded in the French royal accounts for 1404. As the fifteenth century progressed, a number of orders of chivalry, such as the Order of the Golden Fleece of the Duke of Burgundy, were founded, and elaborate collars were provided for the members. Simple gold chains for men are seen in Flemish portraits of the early to middle years of the century.

The hat badge became an accepted part of men's daily costume in the late fifteenth century, and the tradition continued into the sixteenth century. Certain types of jewelry such as earrings are almost unknown, though they are referred to in the *Roman de la Rose,* written about 1300. Curiously, the statue of St. Foy at Conques wears earrings, possibly reflecting the influence of Byzantium on the crusaders. Bracelets, too, are virtually never mentioned, and only a few have survived, such as the one of heart-shaped links with the life of Christ in translucent enamel in the Residenz, Munich.

In the thirteenth century the study of the classical past brought about an interest in cameos and engraved gems. Often used to decorate reliquaries and shrines, they were also occasionally incorporated in personal jewelry. Of the pieces set with cameos of ancient origin, the finest of those surviving is probably the Schaffhausen Onyx, a magnificent first-century

Roman cameo in a German mounting of the mid-thirteenth century. Another example is the lion and dog cameo, with a subject thought to be protection against epilepsy, mounted in a fourteenth-century openwork leaf frame and now in the collection of the Victoria and Albert Museum.

A few superb medieval cameos exist, largely made for the Burgundian court after the fashion of the antique. One is a ring with a portrait cameo of Duke Jean sans Peur of the early fifteenth century, and another is a large brooch with the portrait of the Burgundian courtier Robert de Masmimes. In 1401 the Duke de Berry ordered several rings with his cameo portrait.

Because of the survival of their household accounts, there is considerable information on the finest jewelry made for the kings of France and England and their nobility; however, little of what is documented is preserved. Of the many minor jewels of the citizenry, less is known. Also, they have remained intact only by chance: the medieval jewels shown here were found in drains or mires, where they were lost in medieval times. Most jewelry was melted down for its materials in later times.

As crowns and royal insignia were often dedicated to shrines and cathedrals, many more of them have survived. The reliquary crown of St. Louis, preserved in the Louvre, is replete with cabochon jewels, cast figures of angels in silver-gilt, and filigree. This standard of quality can also be seen in the large religious ring in the British Museum. Set with a toadstone and with a bezel of openwork eagles and a religious inscription, the ring, which was excavated at Cannington, Somersetshire, was probably for an English bishop.

Other religious jewels include rosary beads, which were made of ivory, jet, wood, precious metal, and gemstones. The boxwood paternostre beads of Flanders were famous and widely disseminated in the fifteenth century. Pendants of the fourteenth and fifteenth centuries in translucent enamel on silver and gold are also known, but their fragility and material suggest that only a small proportion of what existed has survived.

The technique of enameled goldwork, which became the standard for pendant jewels in the Renaissance, developed early in the fifteenth century, often taking the form of circular brooches or hat badges in low relief decorated with enamel. The surviving pieces are rather consistent in style and were made largely for the Burgundian court. A famous brooch with two figures in the round is in the Kunsthistorisches Museum, Vienna, and a rare necklace with links in the form of enameled leaves is in the Cleveland Museum of Art.

German traditions favored the gold necklaces of massive scale so well illustrated in the Cranach portraits of Saxon princesses. Often three or four necklaces were worn at the same time. The German merchant class, however, wore simpler jewels of silver-gilt, often of large size, like the Virgin on the sickle moon within a garland of roses (Cat. no. 123).

Mother-of-pearl reliefs were worn in Germany both as ecclesiastical mantle clasps and secular pendants. The designs followed those by the Master E. S. and the Master of the Housebook, and examples exist reflecting known prints. The dissemination of master designs by major artists, made possible by the invention of printing, expanded the goldsmiths' horizon; and the advent of the sixteenth century saw a total change in the approach to jewelry design.

Richard H. Randall, Jr.

Cat. no. 117

117

Clasp or Morse for an Ecclesiastical Vestment

French (Paris), second quarter of fourteenth century
Height: 5¼ in. (13.3 cm)
Width: 5⁷/₁₆ in. (13.8 cm)
Publications: Marie-Madeleine S. Gauthier, *Emaux du Moyen Age Occidental,* Fribourg, 1972, p. 379, no. 146; The Rhode Island School of Design, *Transforma-*

tions of the Court Style, Providence, February 1977, no. 26, p. 79.
Acquired by Henry Walters (?) before 1931. (44.325)

This clasp, a simple quatrefoil, employs three colors of a coarse champlevé enamel on a thin copper ground. Two candle-bearing angels with white enameled details are beneath trefoil arches and flank the Virgin and Child on the plate decorating the pin. They are surrounded with dragons in lozenges of red enamel divided by triangles of red enamel with central white flowers. Three areas of the border have been broken away, including the dragon figure beneath the angel in the left valve, and much enamel is missing. The edge of the clasp is pierced with holes in order to sew it to garments.

The style of this clasp relates to Parisian enamels of the period 1325-50, which include the famous ewer and paten in Copenhagen but more especially the figures surrounding the base of the silver-gilt Virgin of Jeanne D'Evreux of 1339 in the Louvre.

118

Clasp for a Cope or Secular Garment

French (Limoges), late thirteenth century
Height: 3 5/16 in. (8.4 cm)
Width: 4¼ in. (10.8 cm)
Collection of Victor Gay, Sale, Paris, March 23, 1909, lot 35; purchased from Daguerre, New York, 1924. (44.16)

While most of the morses or mantel clasps that have survived from the Middle Ages are clearly of ecclesiastical origin, this example could as well have served to fasten a secular garment. It is carefully made with a

Cat. no. 118

series of holes around the border to sew it to a garment. The original pin, which would have had a large head to make it easy to remove, is missing and has been replaced by a modern one.

The field of each valve is decorated with three cabochon gems in floral settings and a series of large and small stylized flowers carved in intaglio from the copper. The field is blue enamel, leaving the copper-gilt flowers in reserve. The entire clasp is framed in a filed roped border within an outer border of incised petals.

119

Silver Ring Brooch

English, late thirteenth-early fourteenth century
Diameter: 1⅜ in. (3.5 cm)
Purchased from R. Lubin, February 1981. (57.2068)

This silver brooch was found at Tynemouth Castle in 1865. On the front is the inscription IHESUS R(ex), and on the back, "Dug up in graveyard Tynemouth Castle 1865—13th or 14th century." The tongue of the brooch is shaped.

120

Silver Thumb Ring

English, fourteenth century
Diameter: 1¹/₁₆ in. (2.7 cm)
Collection of John Hunt, Dublin; purchased 1969. (57.1989)

This ring is shaped with eight raised facets, which are inscribed IHESUS N in Gothic letters.

121

Signet Ring

German, ca. 1500
Diameter: 1 in. (2.5 cm)
Collection of Melvin Gutman, Sale, Parke-Bernet, May 15, 1970, Part V, lot 121; purchased from Mrs. Ruth Blumka, January 1979. (57.2050)

The faceted hoop of this gold ring is engraved at the shoulders with a man and woman in late-medieval secular dress. Between them on the hoop is plant ornament, now much damaged, and on the facets of the hoop is engraved Gothic foliage. The octagonal bezel has a cabled border, and the signet displays a shaped tilting shield charged with a rampant lion with a billet or flute in his mouth. The lion is surmounted by the initials + S + K +.

122

Pendant Crucifixion

German, late fifteenth century
Height: 2⅜ in. (6.0 cm)
Purchased before 1931. (57.654)

This small cast pendant of silver-gilt shows the Crucifixion with Mary and John. The cross, which is of the rugged type, has a ruby set at the foot and an architectural capital at the base and top. Each capital is attached to a striated ring.

Cat. no. 119

Cat. no. 120

Cat. no. 121

123

Virgin and Child in Glory

German, early sixteenth century
Height: 4¾ in. (12.1 cm)
Collection of Melvin Gutman, Sale, Parke-Bernet, April 24, 1969, lot 11; purchased from L. Blumka, New York, 1970. (57.1991)

The apocalyptic vision of the Virgin and Child in Glory, the so-called "Rosenkranz Maria," was a favorite subject of late Gothic Germany, where it was to be seen in great cathedral chandeliers and miniature objects. The figure of the Virgin is depicted within an aureole of roses. Her feet are on the sickle moon, which surmounts the world; and her head is about to be crowned by angels. The entire vision is seen against a glory of light. The pendant jewel shown here is of cast silver with gilded details and has a roped ring for suspension and another at the base for the attachment of a pendant. The large size of this pendant is due to the emphasis during this period on the necklace as the chief ornament of German women's costume.

Cat. no. 123

Cat. no. 122

124

Pair of Hat Badges

Flemish, early sixteenth century
Diameter of each: 1⅞ in. (4.8 cm)
Purchased before 1931. (45.1-2)

Made in the same workshop, these two silver hat badges with niello decoration show two different styles. One, with the visitation group against a landscape, is based on a fifteenth-century model; the other,

Cat. no. 124

Cat. no. 124

with the Veronica's veil suspended from a dove, shows a more florid early-sixteenth-century style. Originally, each had three loops for attachments, two of which are now missing on the visitation example.

Anthony inscribed IHS beside the Virgin and Child. Each chain passes through a pierced silver ball, and there is an openwork floral hook at the top for suspension. The hook and the bird bear nineteenth-century French tax marks.

Notes: A second example of the Linden prize is in the collection of Museum Vleeshuis (*Schatten van de Vlaanse Schuttersgilden*, Antwerp, 1966-67).

125

Sharpshooter's Prize Medal

Flemish (North Brabant), sixteenth century
Height: 10¾ in. (27.3 cm)
Diameter of medal: 2⅛ in. (5.4 cm)
Length of bird: 3¾ in. (9.5 cm)
Purchased from L. Blumka, New York, 1967. (57.1933)

This medal and bird pendant was the prize for the "king" of a Flemish shooter's guild—the Guild of St. Anthony and the Holy Virgin of the town of Linden, North Brabant. The crowned silver parrot pendant is the symbol of the "king" of the guild and is suspended by silver chains from the guild's medal. Within an engraved border of flowers with the inscription *Sancta Maria Schot van Linden*, the medal shows the Tau of St.

Cat. no. 125

Renaissance Jewelry

During the Renaissance the art of jewelry reached new levels of opulence and artistry, for prodigal expenditure on objects of personal adornment was matched by the genius of goldsmiths whose designs and skills mirrored in miniature the achievements of the age in painting and sculpture. Courtly patronage provided a consistent stimulus, with popes and kings competing for the services of masters such as Benvenuto Cellini and others who adapted the medieval tradition of enameled goldwork to the taste for the glories of the classical past and the exotic splendors of the New World. But although jewelry design was so much affected by the aesthetic inspired by antiquity, there was no attempt to revive archaeological styles or the ancient techniques of filigree and granulation. The change from the Gothic style was principally expressed by deriving surface ornament from relics of Roman pattern called grotesques.

Grotesque motifs came to light in the early years of the sixteenth century, when enterprising artists explored the underground chambers of Nero's Golden House on the Esquiline and those of other palaces, villas, and tombs in other parts of Rome and Naples. Because they were buried so far below ground level, such caverns were known as grottoes, and their stucco and painted decorations accordingly termed grotesques. Light-hearted caprices combining festoons, caryatids, dolphins, masks, cornucopiae, thrysi, pelta shields, hybrids, animals, satyrs, putti, scrolls, and volutes, grotesques were adopted by Raphael and Guilio Romano and applied to the decoration of one of the great Vatican loggias, a loggia which has since provided generations of designers with the most comprehensive array of classical ornament.

Something more substantial, however, was needed as a framework to enclose grotesque ornament, and this was invented during the years 1533-35 by another Italian, Rosso Fiorentino, as a means of framing the series of paintings on the walls of the gallery of François I at the Palace of Fontainebleau. This device, called strapwork, was inspired by decorative leatherwork. Taken up with enthusiasm, especially by the designers of the Low Countries and Germany, it underwent a further transformation under the influence of the oriental arabesque, a stylized plant ornament with winding stem imported into Venice by the Islamic makers of damascened brass. The influence of this type of ornament resulted in the broad scrolls of strapwork being drawn out into narrow and complex interlaced bands known as moresques.

This vocabulary of surface decoration composed of grotesques, strapwork, and moresques was used in decorative gem-set jewels or combined with figure subjects derived from classical and Christian iconography to form ornaments of varicolored enameled goldwork either in relief or wrought in the round. The sculptural and pictorial quality of such pieces as have survived reflects the high standing of the goldsmith and his close connection with other artists. Indeed some of the most celebrated names in Renaissance art—Ghiberti, maker of the bronze Doors of Paradise for the Florence Baptistery, and Verrochio, the teacher of Leonardo da Vinci—were also trained as jewelers. In this atmosphere craftsmen stretched their skills far beyond their traditional limitations, creating little masterpieces to rival those of their colleagues in the major arts. Just as the leadership in architecture, painting and sculpture came from Italy, so did fashions in jewelry; and portraits of courtiers from Venice, Florence, Ferrara, and Milan show that such jewels were made to be worn—to enhance the beauty of hands, hair, neck, and wrists—not to be kept in collectors' cabinets.

Just as the rich in other European countries had already imported Italian examples of the fine arts, so the new style of jewelry went abroad too, and it went first to France. François I invited Benvenuto Cellini to set up workshops for gem engraving under the direction of Matteo del Nazzaro, and in recognition of their importance as symbols of monarchical glory, the king established the collection of French Crown Jewels. The arrival of Catherine de Médicis as the bride of the Dauphin (later Henri II) brought further Italian influence to France, and the style that resulted from this mixture of the French tradition with the Renaissance is exemplified in the beautiful engraved designs for jewels by Etienne Delaune and Pierre Woeiriot.

Because of the Wars of Religion in France, the center of design shifted in the second half of the sixteenth century to the great trading towns of southern Germany—Augsburg, Nuremberg, and Munich. Following the example of Albrecht Dürer, artists from these prosperous centers had studied and traveled in Italy; like him, some also had close family links with the goldsmith's profession. Dürer demonstrated his interest by designing pendants, whistles, and girdle ornaments, while other artists, above all Cranach, faithfully reproduced jewelry in portraiture. The wealth of the banking and commercial families, led by the Fuggers of Augsburg, created a demand for jewels on a scale that encouraged artists to design for a large public. Pattern books were printed, some by Germans such as Virgil Solis (1514-1562) and Matthias Zündt (1498-1586), others by talented Flemings such as Hans Collaert of Antwerp and Theodor de Bry who settled in Frankfurt after 1570—all of them practical craftsmen with some experience of the problems involved.

A remarkable document of the splendor of German Renaissance jewelry was compiled by Hans Mielich, who was employed by Duke Albrecht V of Bavaria to record the treasures of the House of Wittelsbach in an album of miniatures on vellum. Among the jewels illustrated are bracelets, the upper surfaces set with gems in strapwork frames contrasting with the flat backs decorated with interlaced moresques. In Prague, under the patronage of the Emperor Rudolph II (1570-1612), jewelry of equal splendor was produced, epitomized by the imperial crown made by Jan Vermeyen, now in the Vienna Treasury. At the far ends of Europe, both the Hungarian and Spanish courts shared a similar passion for display in clothing and jewels, while across the channel the extravagance of the Tudor household attracted a large colony of foreign goldsmiths and dealers.

Something of the character of the wonderful pieces supplied to Henry VIII and his children and listed in their inventories is revealed in the group of drawings for jewelry by the artist Hans Holbein, who entered the royal service in 1536. Confiscation of the accumulated contents of the church treasuries made quantities of bullion and precious stones available, and courtiers, enriched by grants of monastic lands, had money to spend on jewels, since there were comparatively few other outlets for investment. Queen Elizabeth inherited both the paternal passion for gold and gems as well as the sense of royal power and consistently used jewelry—coronets, necklaces, rings, aglets sewn on her entire dress, and pendants pinned to her ruff, bodice and sleeve—to convey a dazzling image of consecrated virginity and imperial authority. While some of the jewels associated with her are so emblematic that the original meaning has been lost, others contain her portrait or refer to great events such as the defeat of the Spanish Armada.

The international demand, which encouraged artists and jewelers to travel, resulted in a style that became even more cosmopolitan with the diffusion of designs and fashions in dress from France, the Low Countries, and Germany. In addition, the universal taste for classical culture constituted a common market for personal ornaments. Since heads of state were continually exchanging gifts of jewels, it is extremely difficult, in the absence of hallmarks, to establish the place of origin of much surviving Renaissance jewelry. Another issue is the problem of authenticity: most pieces have been repaired, and unlike the examination of paintings by X-rays, there is no scientific means of assessing the extent of such restoration.

Paradoxically, the spirit of intellectual inquiry, which

led to the classical revival and the development of this new style of goldwork, was also responsible for its eclipse: interest in science brought about the improvements in cutting precious stones that culminated in the emergence of the diamond as the principal subject of jewelry. The change is best illustrated by a comparison of the portraits of Henry VIII, resplendent in jewels in enameled settings, and Charles I, discreetly wearing one pearl-drop earring and the diamond-set Badge of the Garter. Although the transition comes almost imperceptibly, a key designer in the process is the Augsburg engraver Daniel Mignot, who around 1600 produced compositions based on the effect of stones juxtaposed into definite forms, independent of the settings. Consequently, the role of the goldsmith was further diminished; for with the elimination of figure work, he had merely to provide settings as unobtrusive as was compatible with fixing the stones securely. Gems, which in the sixteenth-century jewel had been set table cut or *en cabochon* as points of contrast or for their decorative character, continued to assume more and more importance as the art of faceting was mastered, thus releasing all their fire and sparkle. A milestone was the invention of the rose-cut form of faceting, which is displayed in the Lyte jewel given by James I in 1611 to a Somerset squire who had traced the ancestry of the royal house of Stuart back to a refugee from the Trojan War. More encouragement came from the increased supply of diamonds on the market after the opening up of the mines of Brazil and of Golconda in Hyderabad, India. Another influence was Cardinal Mazarin, whose patronage of the lapidaries so stimulated progress that by the end of the century the brilliant cut with thirty-two facets had been discovered.

Because of the Thirty Years' War and threats of invasion from the Turks, Germany lost its prime position in jewelry design, and in the seventeenth century the lead came once again from France. The sense of luxury associated with the diamond accorded well with the concept of absolute monarchy as developed by Louis XIV, and he appeared at the fêtes of Versailles radiant and sparkling in diamond-set parures. Other monarchs used the same formula in order to present an image of transcendent magnificence, and they insisted, in spite of complaints about the oppressive weight of such costumes, that their ladies do the same. Mary of Modena, wife of James II of England, wore jewels valued "at a millions worth, which made her shine like an angel."

So much concentration on glitter meant that jewels could assume simple forms such as bows, stars, rosettes, and knots. The proliferation of them about the person is best described by John Evelyn in his poem "Mundus Mulieribus" published in 1690:

> Diamond buckles too,
> For garters, and as rich for shoo. . . .
> A manteau girdle, ruby buckle,
> And brilliant diamond rings for knuckle. . . .
> A saphire bodkin for the hair
> Or sparkling facet diamonds there;
> Then turquois, ruby, emerauld rings
> For fingers and such petty things
> As diamond pendants for the ears
> Must need be had, or two pearl pears
> Pearl necklace, large and oriental
> And diamond, and of amber pale.

The rococo style of the next century meant that few examples of this diamond jewelry survived remodeling, and information about baroque jewels tends to come from engraved designs or pieces set with pastes, crystals, or marquesite. The designs of Gilles Légaré—court jeweler to Louis XIV—published in his *Livre des Ouvrages d'Orfèvrerie* in 1663, offer an invaluable record. They also illustrate the place of enamel in jewelry of this date: although increasingly relegated to the edges and backs of the majestic gem-set parures represented, it was still the prime means of decoration for watches and miniature cases. The adoption of the method invented by Jean Toutin of Châteaudun meant that their flat surfaces could be painted like pictures in floral designs or miniature versions of landscapes and history painting. Rings, slides for threading onto ribbons to be worn around the neck or as bracelets, could also be enameled in this way; so although almost banished from the settings of the grandest jewels, the technique of enameling, which the Renaissance goldsmith had inherited from his medieval predecessor and brought to perfection in the sculptural jewel, was still, thanks to its renewal by Jean Toutin, holding its own amid the splendors of baroque art.

Diana Scarisbrick

126

Crucifix

Spanish, sixteenth century
Height: 2⁹/₁₆ in. (6.5 cm)
Width: 1⅜ in. (3.5 cm)
Acquired by Henry Walters (?) before 1931. (44.436)

The beveled arms of this enameled-gold rock crystal crucifix terminate in mounts, each of which has four white saltires and finials with studded sunbursts. A nimbed figure of Christ is attached to gold strips. On the back is a relief of the Virgin and Child seated on a column with a black cross. The crucifix has a loop for suspension.

Devotion to Our Lady of the Pillar derives from the tradition that she was transported by angels in 40 A.D. to advise St. James on his mission to Spain. Before returning to Palestine she asked that the marble pillar on which she stood be enclosed in a church dedicated to her at Saragossa.

During the Renaissance jewelry worn at the neck or hanging from chains on the bodice and waist was accorded increasing importance. Following medieval precedent, many pieces of jewelry were religious in character, and chief among them was the cross, for this symbol of Christian faith was considered a powerful talisman. Mary Queen of Scots seems to have always worn one. Rosaries were often extremely luxurious objects, set in gold and bejeweled. They were made in combinations of a variety of materials such as boxwood, jet, rock crystal, coral, amber, agate, and lapis lazuli. Surviving crosses come in an equally wide range of materials and many forms. The Danes and English adopted the Tau cross (shaped like a *T*) symbol of St. Antony Abbot. Another severe form is the Latin cross, sometimes plain but more often with the applied figure of Christ, a scroll inscribed INRI above his head and a skull and crossbones at his feet. Many are engraved with the symbols of the Passion. The Mannerist designs of Virgil Solis (1514-1562) show a softening of the cruciform outline with fronts set with gems in raised lobed collets and backs engraved with arabesques. The gem-studded cross with hanging pearls was intended to equal the splendor of other jewels worn on the person, and in the seventeenth century it attained great magnificence. The gold cross of Lorraine that

Cat. no. 126

Prince Charles presented to the Infanta during his Spanish embassy was set with two rubies and huge diamonds, some of them rose cut, while the cross of Marie de Médicis had a diamond-set crown of thorns and nails, with three additional diamonds hanging in heart-shaped pendants.

Reliquaries represent another large class of devotional jewelry, and crucifixes were sometimes fitted with containers for this purpose. Many were rock crystal pendants that either enclosed miniature representations of devotional images or were decorated in *verre eglomisé*, a technique of painting glass in colors on a ground of gold leaf. Mary Queen of Scots went to her death with a rock crystal Agnus Dei pendant at her neck. Other popular subjects were the Sacred Monogram and the Vernicle, or Holy Face. In addition to reliquaries and rosaries, book pendants containing miniature illuminated manuscripts were worn hanging from the belt.

Cat. no. 127

Cat. no. 128

127
Crucifix

Spanish, sixteenth century
Height: 3 in. (7.6 cm)
Width: 1 15/16 in. (4.9 cm)
Acquired by Henry Walters (?) before 1931. (44.437)

This enameled-gold cross of quadrilobate section, with fleurs-de-lys at the crossing, terminates in reeded finials. The front is blue and green; on the back are white chevrons. The applied nimbed figure of Christ is crowned with thorns. Overhead is a cross inscribed INRI, and below is a jawless skull. Two of the nails and the three hanging pearls are replacements. There is a loop for suspension. The crucifix bears a French control mark.

128
Pendant

Spanish, sixteenth century
Height: 2 11/16 in. (6.8 cm)
Width: 1⅜ in. (3.5 cm)
Publications: "Exhibition of Gold," *BCMA.*
Exhibitions: Cleveland, Cleveland Museum of Art, *Exhibition of Gold,* October 31, 1947-January 11, 1948.
Purchased in Paris, 1927. (44.271)

This enameled-gold and jeweled pendant encloses the crowned Virgin wearing a robe of white brocade and a lined blue star-spangled mantle. The Virgin and the nimbed Infant Christ on her arm (his orb and her sceptre missing) are set within a mandorla with red wavy rays and an outer filigree frame set with diamonds in square collets in the front and colored flower-heads in the back. At the feet of the Virgin are pairs of red flowers on high green stems rising from an oblong reliquary with openwork diamond-set sides and a hinged cruciform base. A scallop shell is applied to the head of the Virgin at the back. The figure of the Child was perhaps added later. There is a loop for suspension. Comparable reliquaries have pendant figures of the Infant Christ and SS. Francis, Jerome, and Antony of Padua, all miniature versions of monumental sculpture.

Cat. no. 129

demand for Hornick's most successful compositions. The pieces reproduced in this way could then be incorporated into settings made to individual choice with gems and pearls or enclosed in rock crystal cases.

130
Pendant

Spanish, late seventeenth century
Height: 1⅞ in. (4.8 cm)
Width: 2⅛ in. (5.4 cm)
Acquired before 1931. (44.509)

This enameled-gold rock crystal pendant encloses a pair of gilded angels venerating the Sacrament on an altar crowned with a baldachino. Forming the frame is a continuous row of beads and a cusped and studded filigree border enclosing trefoils. A filigree octofoil joins the pendant to a rosary of ebony beads. The enameling is all in white with colored detail.

Notes: For another example of this popular subject see Muller, *Jewels in Spain*, fig. 205.

131
Tryptych

European, seventeenth century
Height of each miniature: 2¹¹/₁₆ in. (6.8 cm)
Width of each miniature: 2⅜ in. (6.0 cm)
Acquired by Henry Walters (?) before 1931. (44.311)

This enameled-gold oval tryptych encloses six devotional scenes: the Annunciation, the Adoration of the Shepherds, the Agony in the Garden, the Last Supper, the Crucifixion, and the Resurrection. The rim of the central hinged frame has bead and reel ornament. The rims of the other frames are plain. There is a loop for suspension, and the tryptych closes with a clasp.

The large demand for devotional objects in the Catholic countries could be met by the technique of painting on opaque white enamel, using compositions derived from great masters and diffused through engravings. Examples such as this represent the baroque counterpart of the medieval tryptych.

129
Medallion Pendant

European, ca. 1600
Height: 3⅛ in. (7.9 cm)
Width: 1⅞ in. (4.8 cm)
Purchased from Seligman, Paris, 1906. (44.414)

This enameled-gold and jeweled medallion encloses a varicolored relief of the Resurrection, below which is a diamond-set open tomb, the skeleton of death, and cloven-hoofed Satan. The back, decorated *en suite*, bears the inscription in Roman capitals CIAS (CHRISTUS IESUS ASCENDANS SEPOLCHRO). The frame, with silhouette ornament on a red ground, is embellished with white open scrolls set with diamonds in square collets. Three hanging chains interspersed with pearls are attached to a suspension loop. Three pearls hang below.

Notes: Yvonne Hackenbroch, in her article "Erasmus Hornick as a Jeweller" (*The Connoisseur*, vol. 166, no. 667, September 1967, pp. 54-63), refers to similar medallions in New York, London, and Vienna as exemplifying the practice of using pewter models to meet the

Cat. no. 130

Cat. no. 131

Cat. no. 131

132

Diana Pendant

South German, sixteenth century
Height: 2⅝ in. (6.7 cm)
Width: 2 1/16 in. (5.2 cm)
Publications: John D. Farmer, *The Virtuoso Craftsman*, Worcester Art Museum, March 27-May 25, 1969, no. 60, illustrated; California Palace of the Legion of Honor, *The Triumph of Humanism, Renaissance Decorative Arts 1425-1625*, San Francisco, October 22, 1977-January 9, 1978, cat. no. 97.
Acquired by Henry Walters (?) before 1931. (44.442)

This enameled-gold and jeweled pendant has a scrolled frame that encloses a shell-headed open-arcaded alcove. Framed by baluster columns, the alcove contains a statuette of Diana on a rounded base. She is dressed for the hunt in boots, belted tunic, baldric, and scarf; carries a hunting horn and a bow and quiver; and has a hound beside her. The pendant is set with four table-cut diamonds and five rubies in square collets and has two pearl finials pinned to the outer C-scrolls and three hanging pearls, all replacements. Decorated *en suite*, the back is centered on the alcove facade. There is a loop for suspension.

Besides expressing religious faith and secular intellectual themes, pendant jewels were designed in purely ornamental form. Among the drawings of Hans Holbein are a number of such jewels, and the published engravings of Matthias Zündt and Virgil Solis, dating from the mid-sixteenth century, illustrate the fully developed Renaissance style in elaborate gem-set pendants framed in caryatids and strapwork.

The gems used for this type of pendant, either *en cabochon* or table cut, may have had some additional esoteric significance, since belief in the talismanic power of precious stones was still part of everyday life. While few of these survive, there is a large representation of the type that succeeded them. These have figure subjects enclosed in frames of architectural outline and illustrate the pleasures of hunting, music, and poetry or concepts such as charity and victory. In its final form this style has the architectural elements of the frame set with rows of gems, though these are always subordinate to the setting. Another challenge to the skill of the goldsmith was the introduction of baroque pearls into jewelry. The large irregular shapes inspired a group of pendants of which the harpy pen-

Cat. no. 132

dant (Cat. no. 133) is a splendid example. Well into the eighteenth century pearls continued to suggest witty and sophisticated figures to the goldsmiths of Dresden. The sculptural form of the pendant suited the design of animals and birds, the latter being a Spanish specialty, and also of some legendary hybrids—dragons, sphinxes, and griffins. Appropriately, in the age of the voyages of Sir Francis Drake and the Conquistadores, the sea was another source of inspiration, both in the form of miniature ships complete with crew and passengers and also in a host of maritime creatures.

These large figured pendants took the place of hat badges as the medium through which the virtuosity of the jeweler could be best displayed. They represent the summit of craftsmanship: hammering, casting, chasing, enameling, gem setting, and foiling of the highest quality are combined to produce these miniature works of art. Although the allusions are sometimes obscure, the formula is always the same: gold, enamel, and gems are balanced together so that each element has an equal role in the composition. Further adornment is provided by the luster of hanging pearls and the enameled backs matched by the quality of the gem-set suspension chains. Worn principally by women, pendants hung at the neck, shoulder, or bosom or were pinned to the sleeve, where they could be seen from all sides as they dangled freely.

The international market for such jewels, the publication of designs for them, and the itinerancy of craftsmen makes provenance very difficult to establish, and there was no system of control marks. The wealth of the trading centers of South Germany, Nuremberg, Augsburg, and Munich attracted such numbers of designers and craftsmen that traditionally the figurative pendant in an architectural frame is ascribed to this area, and the style that led to its eclipse also originated there. In Augsburg from 1596 to 1616, Daniel Mignot, a Huguenot, published sets of designs for pendants in three parts: the foundation or back-plate with strictly symmetrical flat scrollwork with holes to which another plate, also with pierced decoration, could be attached with screws, and completing the design, a third section, sometimes enclosing a rosette. It was this multi-layered style studded with gems in high-cusped box collets that dispensed with figure work and led the way to the simplified gem-set pendants of the seventeenth century.

133

Harpy Pendant

Italian, sixteenth century
Height: 2⅜ in. (6.0 cm)
Publications: Randall. ''Jewellery Through the Ages,'' p. 498; Peter Stone, ''Baroque Pearls, part III,'' *Apollo*, vol. 69, 1959, pp. 33, 107.
Acquired by Henry Walters (?) before 1931. (44.486)

The torso of this enameled-gold and jeweled harpy is a baroque pearl. Her head, shoulders, necklace, eagle's wings, fish tail, fins, and legs are chased and colored. The back is decorated *en suite.* Her tail, girdle, and diadem are set with table-cut diamonds; the pendant brooch and fin are each set with a table-cut ruby. The gems are all in square collets. There is a suspension loop and a pendant emerald.

134

Lion Pendant

European, sixteenth century
Height: 2⁷/₁₆ in. (6.2 cm)
Width: 2 in. (5.1 cm)
Publications: Peter Stone, ''Baroque Pearls,'' *Apollo*, vol. 69, 1959, p. 36, fig. VIII; Muller, *Jewels in Spain*, p. 93, fig. 144.
Collection of Canessa, Sale, New York, February 1917, lot 73. (57.618)

The body of this enameled-gold and jeweled lion passant is a baroque pearl. The mane, legs, and twisted tail are chased, and the collar is set with table-cut diamonds in square collets. Two hanging chains are joined to a suspension loop in an enameled flower vase

Cat. nos. 134, 135

Cat. nos. 133, 137 (see colorplate XIV)

set with a table-cut ruby and a triangular diamond. Attached to the vase is a pendant bunch of fruit and flowers.

Although Muller ascribes this jewel to Spain, where the lion is featured in the Royal Arms, it is a heraldic device in other places, notably Venice and Germany, and is used universally as a zodiacal sign and symbol of courage. This quality is conveyed by the threatening pose of the gold head and the muscular force of the baroque-pearl body.

135

Owl Pendant

European, sixteenth century
Height: 4½ in. (11.4 cm)
Width: 2⅛ in (5.4 cm)
Publications: Ada M. Johnson, *Hispanic Silverwork*, New York, 1944, p. 98, fig. 77; Muller, *Jewels in Spain*, p. 96, fig. 156.
Acquired by Henry Walters (?) before 1931. (44.481)

This enameled-gold and jeweled owl *en ronde bosse*, with black and white feathers, grips an openwork varicolored triangular scroll base enclosing birds and leaves. The back is decorated *en suite.* A table-cut tourmaline is set in a raised, central cusped box collet between two small table-cut diamonds in square collets. The back of the owl's head is set with a table-cut ruby in an oval collet; the base, with three table-cut diamonds. Two suspension chains interspersed with stars set with table-cut diamonds (the backs red) are joined to an openwork cartouche set with a cabochon ruby in an oval collet with a hanging pearl and a table-cut emerald in a closed-back fluted collet. Below are two pearls and a ruby, similarly set, and another pearl.

The owl, emblem of Minerva, symbol of wisdom and discretion, is listed in Covarrubias Orozco's *Emblemas Morales* as a device suited for a great captain. Although the openwork base is not of the quality of the bird, this example illustrates the care given to match the decoration of the back to the front of pendants, especially when they are designed to swing from the sleeve, as is this example.

Cat. no. 136

136

Negro Boy Pendant

German (Dresden), early eighteenth century
Height: 2¼ in. (5.7 cm)
Width: 1⅝ in. (4.1 cm)
Acquired before 1931. (57.887)

This silver, jeweled, and lacquered three-quarter-length captive negro boy with hands manacled behind his back is armed with a baroque-pearl helmet, cuirass, and double-hanging pearl pyterges. The cuirass and helmet are bordered with rose-cut diamonds in silver collets. The neck pendant and center of the helmet border are each set with a ruby. His skin is lacquered black, and his eyes are set with red glass. A painted pearl hangs from one ear, and there is a loop for suspension.

Baroque-pearl figurative jewelry, which went out of fashion with the Renaissance pendant, was reintroduced by Johann Melchier Dinglinger (1664-1731) and a Huguenot, Ferbecq, both of whom were goldsmiths to Augustus the Strong in Dresden. Ferbecq is particularly noted for figures incorporating baroque pearls, combining, as in this example, Renaissance ideas with the sophistication and humor of the eighteenth century.

137

Dolphin Pendant

Spanish, sixteenth century
Height: 3⅝ in. (9.2 cm)
Width: 2½ in. (6.4 cm)
Publications: "Arte Colonial en Santo Domingo, Siglos XVI-XVIII," *Unin de Santo Domingo,* vol. 76, no. 1, p. 36, fig. 42; Erwin W. Palm, "Renaissance Secular Jewellery in the Cathedral at Ciudad Trujillo," *Burlington Magazine,* vol. 93, no. 583, October 1951, p. 318, fig. 21; Ann Gabhart, *Treasures and Rarities, Renaissance, Mannerist and Baroque,* The Walters Art Gallery, Baltimore, 1971, p. 26; "Renaissance Objects Installed," *BWAG,* vol. 28, no. 2, November 1975, p. 3, fig. 4; Muller, *Jewels in Spain,* p. 87, fig. 133.
Purchased from Arnold Seligman, Paris, 1929, reputedly from the collection of Baron Alfred C. Rothschild of London. (44.443)

This enameled-gold and jeweled pendant is of a warrior sitting astride a dolphin, whose back is arched in a deep curve and set with six table-cut emeralds in oblong collets. The warrior is wearing boots, a cuirass, and a shako and wielding a long spear. The mouth, eyes, fins, scales, and gills of the dolphin have colored imbricated and guilloche patterns. The back is decorated *en suite.* A hanging pearl and two chains interspersed with red-and-white and green-and-white shields are joined to a double-sided openwork cartouche set with a table-cut emerald. Another pearl hangs below. Attached to the cartouche is a loop for suspension.

Notes: Muller suggests that this may represent Orlando and the Orca, or man-eating whale, from Ariosto's *Orlando Furioso,* Cantos IX and X.

Cat. no. 138

138

Toothpick Pomander

German, sixteenth century
Height: 3³⁄₁₆ in. (8.1 cm)
Publications: California Palace of the Legion of Honor, *The Triumph of Humanism, Renaissance Decorative Arts 1425-1625,* San Francisco, October 22, 1977-January 9, 1978, cat. no. 101.
Acquired before 1931. (44.482)

The openwork convex front of this enameled-gold and jeweled pomander toothpick has pairs of ribbed black cornucopiae, each enclosing a blue quatrefoil, and is set with four table-cut rubies around a central diamond. The gems are set in square collets. The edges are embellished with open scrolls and twin crested eagles' heads with varicolored feathers. The hinged back has black foliate scrollwork down to the plinth and is set with two table-cut rubies. The talon pick issues from the beak of a crested eagle's head (also with varicolored feathers) that terminates in a domed boss. Above are two hanging pearls and a suspension loop.

Although magnificently disguised as jewelry, many Renaissance pendants were designed to serve functional as well as ornamental purposes. Pomanders—scented balls of musk or ambergris placed in hinged and pierced metal containers to be sniffed as a protection against the plague or to counteract unpleasant smells—were used throughout this period because of the poor standards of hygiene. Lord Bacon even recommended them "for the drying of rheums, the comforting of the heart, and the provoking of sleep." First appearing in the shape of an apple or pear, hence the name *pomme d'ambre,* they came as large single containers or in sets like beads. Mary Queen of Scots possessed two of these *accoutrements de senteurs,* that is, a double row of miniature pomanders encircling the head. As a further refinement her earrings contained ambergris.

Other accessories of a practical nature worn in this way were prayer books, mirror cases with brushes attached, ear-picks, whistles, and toothpicks, and in the seventeenth century these took the form of chatelaines with watches and miniature cases added. Occasionally, objects served multiple purposes such as the toothpick pomander shown here.

Toothpicks, in particular, took many shapes and forms. They were not just carried for hygiene and comfort but were worn at the neck or from the waist as highly fashionable adornments (as in Alessandro Oliviero's *Portrait of a Venetian* in the National Gallery of Ireland), and designs for them exist by Heinrich Aldegrever and Erasmus Hornick. One by Hornick is in the form of a mermaid (Johanna Defrates, "Late Renaissance Jewellery," *The Connoisseur,* vol. 190, no. 766, December 1975, figs. 2a, 2b, 4a). Queen Elizabeth owned many toothpicks, one of them a ruby- and diamond-set dolphin and another like a pistol—"a tothe picke of golde made gonne fation." The fashion came to an end with the use of aromatic wood picks, and Shakespeare comments in *All's Well That Ends Well,* Act I, Scene I: "Virginity like an old Courtier wears her cap out of fashion; richly suited but unsuitable, just like the brooch and the toothpick which we wear not now."

139
Esterhazy Marriage Collar

South German or Hungarian, early seventeenth century
Length: 18 in. (45.7 cm)
Publications: "Exhibition of Gold," *BCMA*; Steingräber, *Alter Schmuck,* p. 114, fig. 189.
Exhibitions: Cleveland, Cleveland Museum of Art, *Exhibition of Gold,* October 31, 1947-January 11, 1948.
Collection of Sigmund Bubich, Bishop of Kaschau; purchased from Jacques Seligman, Paris, May 2, 1941.
(44.586)

This magnificent piece is reputedly the collar worn at the wedding of Palatine Miklos Esterhazy in 1611. Assembled from a variety of links, it represents a garland of flowers interspersed with references to love and marriage: the clasped right hands symbolic of trust; the parrots, of docility; the doves, of affection; and the cornucopiae, of the prosperity that comes with marital harmony. With light openwork symmetrical structures enclosing gem-set blossoms, the collar represents the style of the early-seventeenth-century designs of Daniel Mignot. It was this style that introduced the fashion for jewels emphasizing gems rather than sculpture. The enameled-gold and jeweled collar is composed of fourteen pieces—eleven linked in a chain and three pendants—in five different designs, as described below.

The two outer links and central pendant have an openwork scrolled back-plate with white silhouette strapwork. The upper layer is centered on a table-cut ruby in a raised cusped box collet. The base and flanking scrolls are also with white silhouette strapwork. To each side and above and below are gold studs simulating pyramidal-cut diamonds. The lower stud is on a scrolled base supporting a pair of turtle doves beak-to-beak. The outer edges enclose flowers spilling out of cornucopiae, on which perch parrots with multicolored wings and breasts studded with gold simulating triangular-cut diamonds. The parrots frame two right hands clasped with blue cuffs and gold bracelets. They hold a crowned heart from which issues a forget-me-not flower with green leaves studded, respectively, with a gold pyramid and triangle. Pearls with forget-me-not caps hang from the two outer links, and an emerald hangs from the central pendant. The pearls and the emerald are replacements.

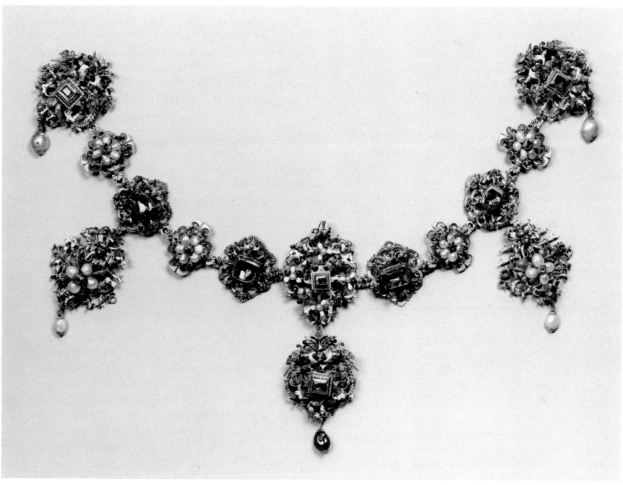

Cat. no. 139 (see colorplate XV)

The two outer pendants have an openwork back-plate of horizontal strapwork with white silhouette or-nament and punched pendant swags. The upper layer is centered on a flower head set with a table-cut diamond in a raised box collet and pinned with four pearls amid varicolored stamen. To each side are table-cut rubies in box collets with black serrated edges; below is a cluster set with two table-cut rubies and a diamond in box collets above a ruby in a petal-shaped collet. The pendant is crowned with a trophy of love emblems: a garlanded, winged flaming heart set with a table-cut diamond, a quiver, a bow and arrow, and a forget-me-not. On either side are links for at-tachments. The modern hanging pearl has a forget-me-not cap.

The four smaller links have a pierced, scrolled shield-shaped back-plate, flanked by white shells en-closing a flower head. The flower head is centered on a table-cut ruby in a high box collet—the base of which has a black serrated edge—pinned with six pearls amid green buds and leaves. The back is channeled for enamel.

The four larger links have a cartouche openwork back-plate with shells above and below linked by monsters with black scaly tails. The upper layer is cen-tered on a large table-cut paste, foiled to simulate a ruby, in a cusped rectangular collet on a base with a black serrated edge within an openwork wreath of eight leafy branches with colored details. The back is channeled for enamel.

The central link has an openwork back-plate of horizontal strapwork and scrolls in white silhouette ornament. The upper layer is centered on a table-cut ruby in a high cusped box collet with a blue-and-white base within an openwork garland of eight flower heads, alternately hexafoils with red and white leaves pinned with pearls, and lilies studded with gold simulating pyramidal-cut diamonds. The garland is crowned with a curved scroll similarly studded in gold.

Notwithstanding the importance of pendants, the chains from which they hung were also a prominent feature of Renaissance jewelry. With or without pendants attached, chains were worn in abundance not only around the neck, but in the hair, across the bodice, and around the waist. They were sometimes enameled and sometimes gem set and had many different types of links. Since they represented capital, the more massive chains were an acceptable means of rewarding service. In the course of the sixteenth century, chains became progressively lighter, culminating in the delicate gem-centered floral links of the type found in the Cheapside Hoard. Although seventeenth-century dress, with its lace trimmings, shimmering satins, and soft lines, was admirably suited to the fashion for long ropes of pearls, and these were therefore worn in profusion, chains still remained an important part of jewelry. The availability of diamonds (due to the opening up of the mines of Brazil and of Golconda in Hyderabad, India) and the progress made in faceting them are reflected in the number of designs for chains with openwork links of chased gold set with rose-cut diamonds.

Portraits provide the best guide to the splendor of jeweled carcanets, or necklaces, formed of small plaques set with stones or ornamented in some other way, like the carcanet of Gabrielle d'Estrées listed in 1599, which consisted of sixteen pieces, seven of them representing the planets. The poet Robert Herrick refers to the more usual formula:

> About thy neck a Carkanet is bound,
> Made of the *Rubie, Pearle* and *Diamond*:
> ("To Julia")

The drawings by Hans Mielich recording the jewelry of Duke Albert V of Bavaria are another source of information; Duke Albert's collar of the Order of St. George, perhaps designed by Mielich and preserved in the Munich Schatzkammer, is the most complete survivor of the type made legendary by the great ruby collar of Henry VIII and those worn on the shoulders of the Magi in paintings of the Epiphany. The necklace shown here and the collar of the Golden Fleece (Cat. no. 140) belong to this splendid category.

140

Collar of the Order of the Golden Fleece

Italian, late sixteenth century
Length of necklace: 28 13/16 in. (73.2 cm)
Height of pendant including pearl: 3 in. (7.6 cm)
Publications: "Exhibition of Gold," *BCMA;* Muller, *Jewels in Spain,* p. 57, fig. 60.
Exhibitions: Cleveland, Cleveland Museum of Art, *Exhibition of Gold,* October 31, 1947-January 11, 1948.
Acquired before 1931. (44.508)

This enameled-gold and jeweled necklace is composed of forty-three links: twenty-one large (in two different designs) and twenty-one small, plus one that links up with the pendant. Each large link is set with a table-cut emerald in a box collet with white dots on a red cartouche pinned with twin pearls (increasing to four after the tenth link) and framed in white openwork bases (alternately of scroll and strapwork) with touches of green, blue, and red. The intervening small links are pierced ovals colored *en suite* and set with a table-cut diamond in a box collet with white dots flanked by twin pearls. The pendant is set with a central hexagonal table-cut emerald in a collet with a white serrated base enclosed in a collar formed of the fire steels and flaming flints of the Golden Fleece and outlined with white dots. Framing the emerald and collar is an openwork ring set with eight table-cut emeralds in box collets with white dots linked with red scrolls and pinned with pearls. Two putti holding flaming torches frame a rose-cut diamond that supports a floriated crown set with three pearls. A pearl hangs from the pendant. The two outer links are joined by a hook and loop.

The Order of the Golden Fleece was founded by Philip the Good in 1430 with the purpose of defending the Catholic faith and liberating the Holy Places, these being symbolized by the motif of the Golden Fleece, while the fire steels and impacting flints are the device

Cat. no. 140

of the House of Burgundy. This necklace compares with another composed of eleven medallions enameled with scenes of the Crucifixion surrounded by the collar of the Golden Fleece and surmounted by a crown, possibly made for the Emperor Rudolph II (1552-1612). The curving outlines, openwork style, and harmony of the varicolored enamels with the gems and pearls, all integrated by the unifying theme of the white dots, suggest a similar late-sixteenth-century date.

Notes: Muller compares the small links with those found in a late-sixteenth-century hoard excavated in Seville (Muller, *Jewels in Spain*, p. 57, fig. 61). For the similar piece mentioned above see Joan Evans, *A History of Jewellery 1100-1870*, New York, 1953, pl. 89.

141

Wedding Crown

Swedish, late seventeenth century
Diameter: 7¾ in. (19.7 cm)
Height: 5⅞ in. (14.9 cm)
Purchased from Ruth Blumka, New York, 1978.
(57.2047)

This silver-gilt crown is adorned with large paste jewels, cast silver ornaments, and stamped flowers of sheet silver. The circlet is framed with raised moldings decorated with punched ornaments, its surface decorated with cast openwork designs set alternately with faceted pastes and silver ornaments imitating pyrami-

Cat. no. 141

dal diamonds. To the upper molding are attached cast silver cherubic heads alternating with flying cherubs.

The major elements of the crown are six cast cartouches of interlaced strapwork, each ornamented with a central paste and four silver flowers. These cartouches are attached to an upper hoop on which are six cast cherub heads with pendant heart-shaped leaves. Six paste jewels are mounted between the cartouches on the upper rim of the circlet. There are eight holes in the circlet to attach the cloth cap.

142

Dress Ornaments

European, ca. 1600
Height of each: ¾ in. (1.9 cm)
Width of each: 1 1/16 in. (2.7 cm)
Acquired before 1931. (57.553-55)

These enameled-gold oval cartouches with black-and-white scrolls entwined around open, punched molded borders are each set with an onyx cameo, the subjects of which are as follows: Hercules strangling the Nemean Lion, two figures in classical dress by an altar with a satyr, and a rustic bringing a goat and fruit for sacrifice (derived from A. Vico, *Monumenta Aliquot Antiquorum ex Gemmis et Cameis incisa,* published in Parma, pl. 5).

Designed to be sewn all over the costume, dress ornaments such as these and those that follow (Cat. no. 143) were another splendid feature of the Renaissance.

Cat. no. 142

Cat. no. 143

These aglets, or appliqués, reflect the style of other jewels and come in the shape of fruit, flowers, snakes, frogs, and cartouches with strapwork frames. They are usually made of enameled gold and set with pearls, foiled stones, or cameos, and sometimes ambergris was inserted into them so the wearer would smell sweetly. The sixteenth-century fashion of huge skirts and sleeves required large sets, and one of the largest belonged to Mary Queen of Scots, who had eighty-four in a pearl-set pattern enameled black and white. In 1605 Anne of Denmark ordered two dozen diamond buttons from the court jeweler Arnold Lulls. This formal taste continued to influence dress ornaments throughout the seventeenth century. Queen Henrietta Maria wears a set of gold doves with diamond breasts in a portrait by Van Dyck. The stomacher, or triangular bodice ornament, was also subject to jeweled enrichment and sometimes had a fan holder attached to the point by a gold or silver chain. Elaborate designs for these in rock crystal and ivory were published by Erasmus Hornick of Nuremberg in 1562.

143

Dress Ornaments

European, sixteenth-seventeenth century
Height of each: 1½ in. (3.8 cm)
Width of each: 1½ in. (3.8 cm)
Acquired before 1931.

These enameled-gold openwork cartouches are set with oval shell cameos. The scenes, all bucolic, are as follows: Pan uncovering a sleeping nymph, a young

Cat. no. 144

faun playing his pipe in a garden of flowers, and a young faun blowing his trumpet. In each setting opaque white dots enliven the color scheme and outline the scrollwork. Each ornament has four loops for sewing onto the costume.

144
Belt Buckles

Hungarian, seventeenth century
Length of each: 9½ in. (24.1 cm)
Width of each: 3 in. (7.6 cm)
Purchased from L. Blumka, New York, March 1972. (57.2000)

These enameled silver-gilt and jeweled belt buckles each have a central panel of openwork arabesques that enclose a huntsman shooting a stag. Set with three jacinth pastes in blue, white, and black curled petal collets, each panel is within an embossed scrollwork border with quatrefoils and beads framed in chainwork. Hinged tongues, decorated *en suite* and set with sapphire pastes in similar petal collets, have snake-head hooks. The openwork arabesques on the sides are set with four turquoise pastes in high round collets. The backs are plain but open for the insertion of a leather or cloth girdle.

Closely connected in style with necklaces are belts, many of them matching and some designed individually. Elizabeth of Valois, wife of Philip II of Spain, is recorded as having a belt made of rock crystal leaves and S-links alternating with enameled-gold branches, and master goldsmith Benvenuto Cellini once made a

marriage girdle three inches wide embossed with small figures. Cellini also writes of another type of belt, made of leather and cloth, for which he designed a silver buckle "the size of a child's head" carved with acanthus, putti, and masks. These buckles, with matching tag ends to hang down in front, had an important place in the costume of the day. In many cases such ornamental fittings were designed to match the sword or dagger, as well as the purse, all of which hung from the belt.

145
Ring with Engraved Gem

Italian, the gem fifteenth-seventeenth century, the setting probably later
Diameter: ¾ in. (1.9 cm)
Height of bezel: 1⅛ in. (2.9 cm)
Collections of Henry Walters before 1931; Mrs. Henry Walters; purchased from Joseph Brummer, New York, 1942. (42.1004)

This plain gold ring has a plasma intaglio with red inclusions. St. Barbara—nimbed, wearing classical dress, and with a martyr's palm in her hand—stands by a miniature tower. The tower has three windows, a reference to St. Barbara's devotion to the Holy Trinity, which led to her martyrdom. In the fifteenth century her image was a talisman protecting the wearer from sudden death.

The combination of engraved gems, either cameos or intaglios, with settings of enameled gold was one of the most successful fashions of the Renaissance. It was

Cat. no. 145

used for pendants and rings, as well as for links for necklaces, bracelets, and belts, and fortunately many of these settings have survived. Some of these cameos and intaglios are ancient, for gems at this time could be picked up daily in the ruins of Rome. Whereas no other jewelry from the classical world had survived in quantity, the gems, which could not be melted down, were still there to provide the link with antiquity. Collections were formed by Pope Paul II and Lorenzo de' Medici, and some gems were worn as jewels. The enthusiasm for gems, both as collectors' pieces and as jewels, stimulated the rise of a school of contemporary engravers whose ambition was to excel the ancients, yet express the spirit of their own time. This meant that gem engraving was closely linked with the style and iconography of monumental sculpture and painting.

Foremost among the classical themes reinterpreted in this way is the portrait, devoid of the abstraction of classical art, yet inspired by the same ideal of human beauty and dignity. Another innovation was the narrative gem, recording events of history and mythology in an anecdotal and detailed manner far removed from the concentrated images of antiquity. From Florence, Venice, Rome, and Milan the art of gem engraving was carried to the Tudor, Valois, and Hapsburg courts, and by 1600, thousands of standardized Lucretias, Cleopatras, Minervas, Cupids, nymphs, and satyrs were being produced to meet the demand. The taste for large sets of such subjects as the twelve Roman emperors encouraged the use of soft substances like shell, which lowered quality still further. The adoption of shiny,

mottled, and banded stones was another encouragement to summary work, since the markings obscured the outline of the engraving. But although gems ceased to be carefully worked, their standing as cultural status symbols was not affected.

Notes: A late-fifteenth-century medieval cameo of St. Barbara is in the Staatliche Sammlung in Munich.

146

Ring with Engraved Gem

Italian, the gem fifteenth-seventeenth century, the setting probably later
Diameter: ⅞ in. (2.2 cm)
Height of bezel: 1¹/₁₆ in. (2.7 cm)
Gift of Laura F. Delano, 1947. (57.1798)

This banded agate intaglio is of Fortune—her hair in a cap and a scarf held up as a sail to the wind—riding on the back of a dolphin. The setting is a plain gold ring.

Cat. no. 146

147

Engraved Gem

Italian, the gem fifteenth-seventeenth century, the setting probably later
Height: 2⁵/₁₆ in. (5.9 cm)
Collections of Henry Walters before 1931; Mrs. Henry Walters; purchased from Joseph Brummer, New York, 1942. (42.1021)

This banded agate intaglio is of Mars—seated and nude except for his helmet—embracing Venus, who stands beside him dangling his shield over her head. The intaglio is a plain gold locket mount.

Notes: This compares with a bronze plaquette in the Kaiser Friedrich Museum, in which the group includes a figure of Cupid. The plaquette is based on a composition by Giovanni Bernardi (1496-1553).

Cat. no. 148

149
Cameo Pendant

European, n.d.
Height: 2⅞ in. (7.3 cm)
Publications: Randall, ''Jewellery Through the Ages,'' p. 499, no. 16.
Collection of Charles Newton-Robinson, Sale, Christie's, June 27, 1909, lot 115. (42.145)

This onyx cameo of a grazing horse is set in a brass pendant with heart-shaped volutes filled with white enamel.

Notes: In quality the cameo compares with fine bronze statuettes of horses, and in iconography, with the rooms in the Ducal Palace of Mantua that are frescoed with the favorite horses in the Gonzaga stables.

Cat. no. 147

148
Cameo Pendant

European, n.d.
Height: 1 in. (2.5 cm)
Publications: Burlington Fine Arts Club, *Exhibition of Ancient Greek Art,* London, 1904, no. M. 181.
Collections of Charles Newton-Robinson, Sale, Christie's, June 27, 1909, no. 95; Morrison, cat. no. 11; purchased from Dikran Kelekian, 1909. (42.139)

This onyx cameo set in a plain gold pendant is of a lion passant.

Notes: This is comparable with the late-fifteenth-century (but possibly ancient) cameo formerly in the collection of Lorenzo de' Medici and now in the British Museum (O. M. Dalton, *Catalogue of the Engraved Gems of the Post-Classical Periods,* London, 1915, no. 32).

Cat. no. 149

150

Pendant Seal

Italian, sixteenth-eighteenth century
Height: 1¹⁵/₁₆ in. (4.9 cm)
Width: 1¹/₁₆ in. (2.7 cm)
Publications: *The Marlborough Gems,* vol. 1, no. 3.
Collections of Earl of Bessborough, cat. no. 19; Duke of
Marlborough, cat. no. 382; Henry Walters before
1931; Mrs. Henry Walters; purchased from Joseph
Brummer, New York, 1942. (42.1083)

Set in a gold mount with openwork handles, this nicolo
intaglio depicts the wreathed head of Julius Caesar
with a star and lituus crook in the field. This type of
Caesar occurs frequently in gems of the sixteenth and
seventeenth centuries, though rarely of this size and
quality.

Cat. no. 150

151

Ring

European, ca. 1600
Diameter: ¾ in. (1.9 cm)
Height of bezel: ¹³/₁₆ in. (2.1 cm)
Publications: *The Marlborough Gems,* vol. 1, no. 18,
London, 1780.
Collections of Lord Chesterfield; Earl of Bessborough,
cat. no. 4C "Nerva"; Duke of Marlborough, cat. no.
509; Henry Walters before 1931; Mrs. Henry Walters;
purchased from Joseph Brummer, New York, 1942.
(42.1038)

The amethyst intaglio of this gold ring is a portrait of a
man. The sides and shoulders of the convex hoop have
foliate scrolls enameled black. The bezel is oval. Admirably characterized in the best Roman tradition, the gem
and the fine ring are well matched.

Perhaps at no other time have rings been worn in
such numbers and made to such high standards as in
the sixteenth century. Intaglios were set in signets,
for seals were needed by all who had business to
transact—nobility, clergy, merchants, lawyers, and private individuals—and each had his personal device.
Cameos were set in decorative rings designed in the
same excellent taste as other jewels—with petal-like
settings of chased and enameled gold and shoulders
with caryatids, volutes, masks, swags, and strapwork.
A further expression of this sculptural character are
those rings with bezels decorated with minute figures
of animals and men *en ronde bosse.*

Many rings were associated with love and marriage—some, with twin hoops, bearing inscriptions
referring to the permanence of matrimony; others,
known as posies, carrying simpler messages, such as *A
Quiet Wife Prolongeth Life.* The symbol of two right
hands clasped appears on rings just as on bracelets and
belts. The devout wore rings bearing the emblems of
faith, and the superstitious carried talismanic rings
made of asses hoof and toadstone. Popes, kings, and
bishops were invested with rings as signs of their authority, and their subordinates wore them as badges of
offices. Pride in possession led to the custom in some

Cat. no. 151

Cat. no. 152

Cat. no. 153

countries, notably Germany, of wearing rings on all fingers, including the thumb, under slashed gloves; and strung on chains in the cap, around the neck, and at the wrist. In the seventeenth century they are worn much more sparingly, designs are simplified, and varicolored sculptural ornament is replaced by floral motifs in black and white. Signets become progressively lighter, and the fashion for wearing intaglios in pendant seals hanging from the waist rather than in rings is introduced. The development at the end of the seventeenth century of multiple faceting of gems and the subsequent invention of brilliant cutting was accompanied by the increased use of precious stones, especially the diamond, set either in cluster or solitaire.

152
Ring

European, sixteenth century
Diameter: 1 in. (2.5 cm)
Acquired before 1931. (44.313)

The raised box bezel of this enameled-gold ring is on

an inverted truncated pyramid set with a table-cut diamond and supported by six eagles' talons. Openwork shoulders enclose grotesque masks. The hoop is convex.

153
Papal Ring

Italian, fifteenth century
Height: 1½ in. (3.8 cm)
Acquired before 1931. (54.433)

The oblong bezel of this bronze-gilt ring is set with a foiled crystal in an arcaded collet. On the sides are symbols of the Evangelists in high relief with pairs of shields between them. On the round hoop are a *biscione* and a double-headed eagle. The *biscione*, the device of the Milanese families of Sforza and Visconti, is a large snake with a child in its mouth.

Notes: For a similar example in the British Museum, see O. M. Dalton, *Catalogue of the Finger Rings*, London, 1912, no. 850.

154

Ring

European, late sixteenth century
Diameter: 13/16 in. (2.1 cm)
Height of bezel: 9/16 in. (1.4 cm)
Collections of Lord Chesterfield; Earl of Bessborough,
cat. no. 104 "Julia Pia Felix"; Duke of Marlborough,
cat. no. 472. (42.1071)

The carnelian intaglio of this gold ring is a portrait of
Faustina the Younger, wife of Marcus Aurelius (died
A.D. 175). Scrolls enameled black are on the shoulders
and sides of the bezel. The hoop is square.

Cat. no. 155

Cat. no. 154

155

Pair of Earrings

French, seventeenth century
Height: 2⅛ in. (5.4 cm)
Acquired before 1931. (44.522-23)

Designed as eight-pointed stars, these enameled-gold
and jeweled earrings are set with table-cut diamonds in
square collets. The points are linked by arcs with black
dots on a pale blue ground. The backs are decorated *en
suite*. The pearls above and the hanging pearls are all
replacements. The earrings bear French control marks.

Earrings were a favorite form of jewelry for both men
and women in Renaissance times. One of the diamond-set marten's heads listed in the inventory of

Marie de Médicis had pearl earrings, and the Queen
herself was very partial to this form of jewel, reserving
her best diamonds (in one instance set in a pair of
miniature crowns) for wearing on her ears. Earlier earrings were the vehicle of sixteenth-century fantasy
and were made in designs as varied as negro heads,
Jerusalem crosses, rock crystal lions, and even twin-
tailed lute-playing mermaids. In the seventeenth century design becomes less individual. Pearls are almost
ubiquitous, though in Spain long emerald-set pendants
were favored, and another popular form, the diamond
and pearl ribbon and chandelier type, was published by
Gilles Légaré in 1663. For some time they were worn
by men: Henry III of France owned a pair of diamond
earrings, and Charles I went to his execution wearing
the single pearl drop now in the collection of the Duke
of Portland. Unfortunately, it was the usual fate of
earrings to be refashioned to suit the taste of later
wearers, and few examples have survived.

Cat. no. 156

Cat. no. 156

156

Memento Mori Watch

German, early seventeenth century
Height: 1⅞ in. (4.8 cm)
Collection of Anatole Demidoff, Prince of San Donato;
purchased from Tiffany & Co. (58.42)

The jaws of this metal-gilt skull watchcase open to a
silver dial framed in continuous scrollwork. The top-
plate is inscribed JOHAN PLANG INN G(R) AT. The case
has a ring for suspension.

157

Flowered Watch

French (Paris), seventeenth century
Diameter: 2⅛ in. (5.4 cm)
Publications: Philippe Verdier, ''Seventeenth-century
French Enameled Watches,'' *Antiques,* vol. 84, no. 6,
December 1963.
Collection of Anatole Demidoff, Prince of San Donato;
purchased from Tiffany & Co., 1893, list no. 36.
(58.148)

This enameled-gold round watchcase is decorated on
the back with a bouquet of mixed flowers in pink
grisaille outlined in gold on a translucent green ground.
The dial center is decorated *en suite* and framed in a
black-and-white scalloped border. The inside of the
back has a varicolored bouquet and birds on a
white ground. The top-plate is inscribed G. GAMOD
A PARIS. The watch has a ring for suspension.

In the seventeenth century, watches which in early
Renaissance times had assumed a wide variety of
forms, including the memento mori skull, were enclosed in more convenient round cases, the plain outline and regular surfaces of which opened up new
possibilities for the enameler. At the turn of the century, designers, among them Stephen Carteron and
Michel Le Blon, transformed the curves of arabesques
and strapwork into broken stylized patterns outlined
in gold on single color grounds. Sometimes called
schwarzornament, this silhouette style was followed by
peapod patterns. Published by Pierre Marchant and
Balthaser Lemersier, these patterns were derived from
pods, husks, and leaves, and with them came the taste
for naturalism stimulated by the opening of the Jardin
des Plantes in Paris. Botany was the theme of a series of
pattern books issued between the publication of the
Livre des Fleurs by François Léfebure in 1639 and the
Livre des Fleurs Propres pour Orfèvres by Jean Vauquer
in 1680, and although the lead came from France,
others made important contributions, notably the
Nuremberg designer Johannes Heel.

Notes: The case compares with another in the Victoria and Albert
Museum ascribed to Henri Toutin (1614-1683) of Blois, which combines champlevé and painted enamel in a similar naturalistic floral
design, in the style of Jean Vauquer. The watchmaker, Gregoire
Gamod, was established in Paris on the Rue de la Barillerie from 1652
to 1673.

Cat. no. 157 (see colorplate XVI)

Cat. no. 157 (see colorplate XVII)

Cat. no. 157

Eighteenth- to Early-Twentieth-Century Jewelry

The eighteenth century saw a decline in colored enamels and an increase in the use of diamonds and other faceted gems and glass paste substitutes, especially in jewelry intended to be worn in candlelight. Following the prevailing fashion, jewelry vividly reflected the asymmetrical, naturalistic rococo style in the second quarter of the century and the more restrained neoclassical style in the succeeding decades.

Chatelaines, a popular form of eighteenth-century jewelry, were intended for daytime and evening and were worn by men and women. A French example of about 1769 (Cat. no. 159), together with a pendant watchcase, exemplifies the pictorial use of quatre-couleur gold, in which various colors were achieved with different alloys—copper for red, silver for green, iron for yellow, and silver or platinum for white. Other chatelaines, both French and English, are decorated with pictorial scenes in painted enamels. In the nineteenth century chatelaines returned to fashion in the romantic era of the 1830s, at mid-century, and again in the 1870s.

A collection of rings, purchased by Henry Walters in Paris as a present for his sister, documents the changing styles in this form of jewelry. Several of the earliest eighteenth-century rings are of the cluster type, in which the circular bezel is set with a central stone surrounded by smaller stones; others, dating from the third quarter of the century, share distinctive, large openwork bezels set with stones or pastes; and a significant portion adhere to the marquise type of the end of the century. Derived from the laurel leaf of classical jewelry, the elongated shuttle-shaped bezel of the marquise ring is faced with an enameled plate, usually a translucent deep blue, surrounded by a border of diamonds or pastes and set with a centralized decorative motif also rendered in diamonds or pastes. The marquise ring occurs widely in continental European jewelry at the turn of the century and subsequently proved in France to be a remarkably enduring form through much of the nineteenth century. Other neoclassical rings, set with intaglios and cameos of both ancient and modern origin, reflect the enthusiasm for gem-carving, which had waned in the preceding century but was revived in the late eighteenth century and flourished during much of the nineteenth century.

The impact on jewelry production of the Industrial Revolution, first apparent in England, is manifested in such pieces as the pair of belt clasps (Cat. no. 176) in which Wedgwood ceramic medallions have been substituted for cameos and set in manufactured cut-steel frames with faceted studs simulating jewels.

To meet the market created by the affluent middle classes of nineteenth-century Europe and America, the decorative arts were increasingly mechanized. In jewelry it was more often the manufactured secondary jewelry, rendered with materials of minor intrinsic value, rather than the primary, gem-set precious pieces, that more vividly reflected fluctuations in fashion.

With the establishment of the First French Empire,

Paris again reassumed her role as an arbiter of taste. Cameos inspired by ancient prototypes became fashionable and were worn in various forms including diadems and clasps, as depicted by J. L. David in his *Coronation of Napoleon I* in the Louvre. This fashion encouraged Napoleon to introduce in 1805 a *prix de Rome* for engravers of fine stones. The cameo representing the Empress Josephine (Cat. no. 178) carved by Teresa Talani, who was noted for her images of the imperial family, is a fine example of this style.

With the end of the Napoleonic Wars and a return to relative prosperity, the art of jewelry flourished. The use of precious stones, which were more readily available, and an emphasis on naturalistic motifs characterized the jewelry of the 1820s and 1830s.

Secondary jewelry of the 1830s is exemplified by the elaborate parure (Cat. no. 183), in which half-pearls, diamond chips, and small emeralds have been set in patterns over the enameled surfaces of a hollow framework of thin machine-stamped gold. Here, the effects of display and color have been maximized with materials of modest intrinsic worth and a minimum expenditure of labor.

Much English and American secondary jewelry was sentimental or associated with mourning. In the closing years of the eighteenth century, there evolved a vocabulary of motifs including urns, broken columns, weeping willows, grieving widows, and orphans that replaced the earlier, more macabre memento moris. A rather conventional example is the American ring of the 1820s (Cat. no. 180) with a bezel bearing the figure of Hope painted in sepia on ivory, encased beneath a crystal, and surrounded by a border of small crystals. An earlier, more distinguished ring (Cat. no. 179), commemorating the deaths of A. E. and C. M. Burnley in 1803 and in 1804, is separated transversely, with the two hoops held together by tiny pins and sockets. Each half of the bezel divides to form a triangular member in which plaits of hair are mounted.

Initially, in sentimental jewelry the hair of the beloved or deceased was used in locks and plaits or worked pictorially and enclosed in various frames, including lockets and the backs of miniatures and rings, but by the 1840s it was being braided and woven into a number of shapes, such as the necklace and pendant cross composed of woven spheres of hair (Cat. no. 181).

Long periods of mourning were rigidly observed, with Queen Victoria setting a precedent by grieving for her husband, Albert, from 1861 until her own demise in 1901. As a result, in the second half of the century, suites of jewelry evolved made of such somber materials as onyx, jet, and black glass.

Foreign travel was growing more financially feasible and convenient for an ever-increasing number of individuals. Many of the travelers' purchases abroad fall within the category of "souvenir jewelry." Shown here are a horn brooch (Cat. no. 188) delicately carved with a hunting scene from Germany; several examples of so-called "peasant" jewelry from France, in which traditional forms have been retained long after they had fallen out of fashion in the urban centers; and a variety of works from the Italian states, all of which could be classified as souvenirs. From Naples and Genoa came quantities of coral, said to have been popularized by the marriage in 1845 of the Duchesse d'Aumale to the Prince of the Two Sicilies. Turned in beads or carved into pseudo-classical heads and foliate forms, the coral was mounted in parures and individual brooches and bracelets. Miniature glass tesserae mosaics showing traditional scenic views were manufactured in the Vatican workshops for various jewelry firms. The engraving of cameos, in hard stone or shell, which had initially been directed towards a limited market of wealthy cognoscenti, increasingly became a branch of the tourist trade for Rome, Florence, and Naples. Early in the century Pope Leo XII opened a public school devoted to cameo and medal engraving in the Ospizio di San Michele in Rome. At the 1862 International Exhibition the Vatican was represented by the displays of six cameo carvers.

In some countries it was the Middle Ages, rather than classical antiquity, that drew the attention of designers. The vigor of the Gothic revival in Austria is exemplified by the elaborate gold bracelet formed of five ogival arches set with various colored stones (Cat. no. 185).

At the turn of the century, Henry Walters made a number of diverse purchases of contemporary jewelry. From the Tiffany & Co. exhibit at the Exposition Universelle of 1900, he bought a large corsage ornament in the form of an iris naturalistically rendered in American sapphires (Cat. no. 206). The piece not only exemplifies the opulence of much precious jewelry of the period but, more specifically, illustrates a commitment to indigenous gems on the part of George F. Kunz, director of the celebrated firm's Jewelry Department.

A more *retardataire* purchase was a collection of gold intaglio-mounted necklaces and bracelets from Giacinto Melillo in Naples in 1903 (Cat. nos. 195-97). Melillo, a former employee of Alessandro Castellani, continued well into the twentieth century to produce archaeological jewelry with the characteristic granulation and filigree popularized by the Castellanis in the middle of the previous century.

More spectacular was a selection of pieces purchased at René Lalique's exhibit *Objets et bijoux d'art* at the Saint Louis World's Fair in 1904. Lalique, working in a style that was in many respects directly antithetical to that of the Tiffany iris brooch, dominated French art nouveau jewelry production. For textural and coloristic effects, he introduced novel substances such as bone and horn, combining them with an array of precious and semiprecious materials to create works that were frequently more appropriate for display than for being worn. The examples shown here (Cat. nos. 209-13)

date from relatively late in Lalique's career as a jewelry designer, when he had evolved a naturalistic style that was more personal than typically art nouveau. He was at this point turning increasingly to glass, a medium he was soon to adopt as his primary means of expression.

In the post-World War I era a number of artists distinguished for their work in other media drew designs for jewelry that was to be realized by the artisan. However, the jewelry trade of the twentieth century has been dominated by large firms employing designers who for the most part have remained anonymous, a development that had been anticipated by Tiffany & Co. As a result, much present-day commercial jewelry has been restricted to the setting of faceted gems with limited artistry. The role of the independent designer-craftsman responsible for the conception and execution of his designs has received insufficient attention, though a resurgence in his role has now become discernible.

William R. Johnston

Cat. no. 158

158

Watch

Swiss, 1840s
Height: 2⅝ in. (6.7 cm)
Collection of Henry Walters before 1931. (58.110)

A watch movement with a white enameled dial encircled by brilliants has been inserted in the center of a pectoral cross. The face of the cross is set with a tooled gold ground painted in enamels with a half-length Virgin and Child, the young St. John the Baptist, and two pairs of cherub heads. Engraved on the reverse of the cross is a Latin inscription from St. Luke I:28-30, in which the Archangel Gabriel addresses Mary. Surmounting the cross is a ring with a loop for suspension.

159

Chatelaine

French (Paris), 1769
Height: 7¼ in. (18.4 cm)
Collection of Anatole Demidoff, Prince of San Donato, Sale, New York, Tiffany & Co., 1893, lot 84. (57.881)

Rendered in chiseled gold with inlays in quatrecouleur, this chatelaine was made by Jean Louis Baron, who was active from 1748 to about 1792. From the upper triangular hook-plate is suspended a row of four plaques connected by circular links. Running between the hook-plate and the bottom plaque, on each side, is a row of three S-shaped scrolls, also connected by links. Two identical scrolls hanging from the corners of the hook-plate terminate in swivel hooks. Both the plate and the suspended plaques are decorated with circular and oval musical and pastoral trophies on striated grounds. A loop has been soldered to the hook for purposes of display. The chatelaine bears the warden's mark F for 1769; the *fleur fleuronné* and the helmeted head of the fermier Julien Alaterre (1768-74); and the initials J. L. B. with a crown for the maker, Jean Louis Baron.

Chatelaines usually consisted of a top-plate from which hung series of chains supporting smaller plaques that in turn carried hooks for various devices. The top-plate was backed with a large flat hook used for suspending the chatelaine from the waist of the wearer. Watches and signet seals often hung from chatelaines for men, whereas *étuis,* watches, and sewing accessories hung on those for women.

Notes: Presently suspended from the chatelaine is a watch of similar style (acc. no. 58.45) with a case in quatrecouleur gold. Shown in an oval medallion is a seated hunter with his dog and some game. The case bears the warden's mark B for 1765-66; the crossed branches of the fermier Jean-Jacques Prevost (1762-68); PDM for the maker; and the incised number 9305. The dial is signed *Filon/ A PARIS.*

160

Chatelaine with Watch

French, eighteenth century
Height: 6¹⁵⁄₁₆ in. (17.6 cm)
Acquired before 1931. (58.16)

This metal-gilt chatelaine is comprised of a hook-plate with three plaques hinged together and two lateral

Cat. no. 159

Cat. no. 160

pendants, on one of which is suspended a watch-key and on the other, a revolving seal of rock crystal. The seal, which is not engraved, is set in a mount formed by two dolphins and a mask. Neither the seal nor the key appear contemporaneous with the chatelaine and watch. The decoration of the chatelaine and outer

watchcase consists of garlands and scrolls of metal-gilt in a symmetrical pattern over panels of striated agate.

Notes: The back-plate of the watch is engraved *frs. Melly à Paris.* Tardy cites *Melly frères à Paris* on a Louis XVI clock (*Dictionnaire des Horlogers français, Paris,* n.d., p. 453).

Cat. nos. 161, 162, 163

161

Ring Watch

French, ca. 1780
Diameter of hoop: ¾ in. (1.9 cm)
Diameter of dial: ¹⁷/₃₂ in. (1.4 cm)
Collection of Anatole Demidoff, Prince of San Donato,
Sale, New York, Tiffany & Co., 1893, lot 54. (58.50)

The white watch dial is surrounded by a ring of brilliants. These stones are also mounted to form floral
sprays on the pierced shoulders of the gold ring.

162

Brooch Watch

Swiss, early nineteenth century
Height: ¹⁵/₁₆ in. (2.4 cm)
Width: ⅝ in. (1.6 cm)
Collection of Anatole Demidoff, Prince of San Donato,
Sale, New York, Tiffany & Co., 1893, lot 46. (58.53)

The gold case is rectangular with cut corners and is
bordered with small pearls. Inset in the blue steel face
are the watch dial and a balance set with brilliants.
The back of the case bears the inscription *Tournez les
E . . . illes/Rémontés/a gauche* and the initials R. A.

Notes: A similar watch equipped with automata and mounted as a
bracelet is illustrated in Eugène Jaquet-Alfred Chapuis, *La Montre
Swisse*, Basle and Olten, 1945, pl. 89.

163

Mandolin Watch

Swiss (?) with Austrian movement, early nineteenth
century
Height: 2⁷/₁₆ in. (6.2 cm)
Acquired before 1931. (58.34)

Switzerland was noted at this time for novelty watches
in which the movements were incorporated into a variety of jewelry forms. In this example the movement is
mounted in a mandolin-shaped gold brooch that opens

to reveal the dial. The sound board of the mandolin is divided into zones of red and cream-colored enamel. The interior is blue enamel. A double chain is attached for suspending the brooch. The back-plate bears the inscription *Franz Schmit in Gratz.*

Notes: Similar novelty watches are illustrated in Eugène Jacquet-Alfred Chapuis, *La Montre Swisse*, Basle and Olten, 1945, pl. 87.

164
Ring

English, eighteenth century
Diameter: $^{11}/_{16}$ in. (1.8 cm)
Collection of Henry Walters; Laura F. Delano; gift of Laura F. Delano, 1946-47. (57.1799)

This gold ring with silver collets has a crowned, reeded heart-shaped bezel set with diamonds. The channeled hoop has foliate split shoulders, each of which encloses a cinquefoil.

165
Ring

English, mid-eighteenth century
Diameter: $^{9}/_{16}$ in. (1.4 cm)
Collection of Henry Walters; Laura F. Delano; gift of Laura F. Delano, 1946-47. (57.1778)

This gold ring with silver collets has a square, reeded bezel set with three table-cut diamonds. The ribbed hoop has forked shoulders similarly set.

166
Ring

Italian, early eighteenth century
Diameter of hoop: ¾ in. (1.9 cm)
Diameter of bezel: ⅝ in. (1.6 cm)
Collection of Henry Walters; Laura F. Delano; gift of Laura F. Delano, 1946-47. (57.1766)

The octofoil bezel of this gold ring is set with radiating table-cut diamonds. The channeled hoop has forked shoulders, each of which is set with a small diamond. The ring bears the Paris mark ET, introduced in 1864 for gold imported from countries without customs conventions.

Cat. nos. 164, 165, 166

167
Ring

French or Spanish, 1770
Diameter: ⅝ in. (1.6 cm)
Height of bezel: 1¼ in. (3.2 cm)
Collection of Henry Walters; Laura F. Delano; gift of
Laura F. Delano, 1946-47. (57.1762)

The openwork octagonal bezel of this gold ring with
silver collets has a jadeite (?) cameo mask and is inlaid
with gold amid tied diamond-set palmettes within a
border similarly set. The ribbons are set with rubies.
The wire hoop has split shoulders, each of which encloses a diamond-set trefoil.

168
Ring

Spanish (?), second half of eighteenth century
Diameter: 9/16 in. (1.4 cm)
Length of bezel: 1⅛ in. (2.9 cm)
Collection of Henry Walters; Laura F. Delano; gift of
Laura F. Delano, 1946-47. (57.1791)

Set with diamonds, this gold ring with silver collets has
an openwork marquise bezel with a wreathed central

vesica enclosed within a plain border. The wire hoop
has pierced scrolled shoulders.

169
Ring

Spanish, second half of eighteenth century
Diameter: 9/16 in. (1.4 cm)
Length of bezel: 1 1/16 in. (2.7 cm)
Collection of Henry Walters; Laura F. Delano; gift of
Laura F. Delano, 1946-47. (57.1788)

This gold ring, set with diamonds in silver collets, has a
lozenge bezel with an openwork cruciform center amid
leaves within a plain border. The channeled hoop has
pierced scrolled shoulders.

Cat. nos. 167, 168, 169

Cat. nos. 170, 171

170

Ring

French, ca. 1770
Diameter: ¾ in. (1.9 cm)
Height of bezel: 1⅛ in. (2.9 cm)
Collection of Henry Walters; Laura F. Delano; gift of
Laura F. Delano, 1946-47. (57.1790)

The octagonal bezel of this gold ring with silver collets
has a diamond-set bird and branch on a foiled dark blue
enameled ground within a diamond-set border. The
bird's eye is set with an amethyst. The plain hoop
expands at the shoulders.

171

Ring

European, late eighteenth century
Diameter: ⅝ in. (1.6 cm)
Height of bezel: 1¹/₁₆ in. (2.7 cm)
Collection of Henry Walters; Laura F. Delano; gift of
Laura F. Delano, 1946-47. (57.1751)

The rectangular bezel of this gold ring with silver collets
has a diamond-set basket of flowers on a foiled dark
red enamel ground within a diamond-set border. The
plain hoop expands at the shoulders. The ring bears a
weevil in an oval, a mark introduced in 1864 for gold
imported from countries with customs conventions.

172

Ring

French, 1770-1800
Diameter: ¾ in. (1.9 cm)
Length of bezel: 1¹³/₁₆ in. (4.6 cm)
Collection of Henry Walters; Laura F. Delano; gift of
Laura F. Delano, 1946-47. (57.1763)

The lozenge bezel of this gold ring with silver collets
has a diamond-set galaxy centered on a solitaire on a
foiled dark blue enamel ground within a diamond-set
border. The forked shoulders of the convex hoop each
enclose a leaf.

Cat. no. 172

Cat. nos. 173, 174, 175

173

Ring with Sardonyx Cameo

French, late eighteenth century
Diameter: 11/16 in. (1.8 cm)
Height of bezel: 3/4 in. (1.9 cm)
Collection of Henry Walters; Laura F. Delano; gift of
Laura F. Delano, 1946-47. (57.1787)

The oblong bezel of this gold ring with silver collets has
a sardonyx cameo portrait of Queen Marie Antoinette
and the Dauphin of France within a border of diamond
sparks. Each of the forked shoulders of the channeled
hoop encloses a tulip set with a diamond (one missing).

174

Ring with Sardonyx Cameo

Italian, eighteenth century
Diameter: 3/4 in. (1.9 cm)
Height of cameo: 1 1/16 in. (2.7 cm)
Collection of Duke of Marlborough, cat. no. 14; pur-
chased by Henry Walters at Joseph Brummer sale, New
York, 1942. (42.1197)

This gold ring has a sardonyx cameo of the wreathed
head of Jupiter within a raised border with beveled
edges. The oval bezel has a clipped rim and an open
back. The hoop is channeled.

175

Ring with Gold Relief

Italian, late eighteenth century
Diameter: 11/16 in. (1.8 cm)
Height of bezel: 13/16 in. (2.1 cm)
Collection of Duke of Marlborough, cat. no. 184;
purchased by Henry Walters at Joseph Brummer sale,
New York, 1942. (42.1220)

A molded gold relief of Perseus holding the head of
Medusa has been set against a dark, rough iron
ground. This technique served as an alternative to re-
producing engraved gems in glass or ceramics. The oval
bezel has a raised edge and is attached to a plain hoop.

176

Pair of Belt Clasps

English, 1780-1800
Height overall: 3 5/16 in. (8.4 cm)
Height of medallions: 2 17/32 in. (6.4 cm)
Width overall: 2 1/4 in. (5. 7 cm)
Purchased by William and Henry Walters in Vienna,
1878. (48.1770-71)

A pair of elliptical Wedgwood blue-and-white jasper
medallions has been set in cut-steel frames. The use of
faceted cut-steel studs to simulate jewels occurred as

Cat. no. 176

early as the seventeenth century in the production of ornamental sword hilts, and in the eighteenth century the practice was applied to jewelry. When used in conjunction with Wedgwood's ceramics, it is generally associated with a factory established by Matthew Boulton in Birmingham in 1764. In the frames shown here the filed and polished studs have been individually mounted on a base-plate of tin. Portrayed on the medallions are scenes of sacrificing classical priestesses identical to those occurring on a tablet designed by Lady Templeton and Miss Crewe for Wedgwood's fac-

tory, Etruria, as noted in Eliza Meteyard's *Memorials of Wedgwood,* London, 1874, pl. XXIV.

177

Necklace

French, late eighteenth century
Length: 17½ in. (44.5 cm)
Gift of Saidie A. May, 1945. (57.1738)

With the disruption of the economy in the late eighteenth century, there arose in France a fashion for

Cat. no. 177

jewelry rendered in non-precious metals. This neoclassical copper-gilt necklace is composed of a chain of flat wire links with subordinate loops, from which hang pendants in the form of spheres with rounded arrowhead drops.

178

Pendant with Cameo Portrait of the Empress Josephine

Italian, ca. 1797
Height overall: 1 9/16 in. (4.0 cm)
Publications: Anonymous, *The Walters Collection*, Baltimore, 1895, p. 102, no. 188; and subsequent Walters' catalogues.
Acquired with several miniatures by William T. Walters, through George A. Lucas, from the Paris dealer Philippe Sichel in 1892. (42.202)

The work of Teresa Talani, this shoulder-length profile of the Empress Josephine is carved of white-and-grey agate. The cameo is mounted in a finely chased gold frame with a blue enameled inner border, and a loop has been applied for suspension. At the bottom is the name (TE)RESA TALANI.

Cat. no. 178

In a letter of July 27, 1892, to George Lucas, William Walters' friend and advisor Philippe Sichel reported that this pendant and the other objects purchased with it belonged to the Marquis A. Biron, who inherited them from his grandmother, the wife of Marshall Henri-Gratien Bertrand (1773-1884), who had accompanied Napoleon to Saint Helena.

Notes: L. Forrer in *Biographical Dictionary of Medallists* (vol. 6, London, 1916, pp. 8-9) mentions an agate cameo of Josephine and Napoleon by this gem-carver of Roman extraction who worked in Naples.

179
Mourning Ring

English, ca. 1803-1804
Diameter: ¾ in. (1.9 cm)
Acquired before 1931. (44.528)

This bipartite ring bears on its hoop two inscriptions in gold lettering against a white enamel ground banded in black: C.M.BURNLEY. DIED. 3 MAR. 1804. AGED 19 and A.E. BURNLEY. DIED. 8 JULY 1803. AGED 20. The white enamel ground signifies that the deceased were unmarried. The bezel consists of two triangular sections, each containing a plait of hair beneath glass, framed with small white and grey pearls. The hair of the elder brother was dark brown and the pearls employed are white, whereas the younger brother had light brown hair, which is shown with grey pearls. The two sections of the ring are held together by a pair of small pins and sockets.

180
Mourning Ring

American, ca. 1820
Diameter: $^{13}/_{16}$ in. (2.1 cm)
Height of bezel: 1 in. (2.5 cm)
Gift of Mrs. Charles E. Rieman, 1958. (57.1875)

Mounted with a convex crystal and set with small brilliant-cut crystals, the large oval bezel of this gold ring bears a miniature in sepia on ivory showing Hope with her anchor.

181
Hair Necklace and Pendant Cross

English, ca. 1850
Length of necklace: 18¼ in. (46.4 cm)
Height of cross: 1$^{15}/_{16}$ in. (4.9 cm)
Anonymous bequest, 1970. (57.2046)

A pendant cross composed of six spheres of woven hair connected with thin gold loops hangs from an embossed and chased hollow gold clasp set with a faceted garnet. The necklace is made of loops of braided horsehair interspersed with sections of flat gold links.

182
Mourning Brooch

English or American, ca. 1850
Height: ¾ in. (1.9 cm)
Width: 1$^{5}/_{16}$ in. (3.3 cm)
Gift of Mrs. Sara D. Redmond, March 1979. (57.2060)

This oval brooch of low-grade gold bears a woven braid of brown hair beneath a crystal. The face of the brooch is decorated with a machine-stamped braided border.

Cat. no. 179

Cat. nos. 180, 181, 182

Cat. no. 183

Cat. no. 184

183

Parure

French, ca. 1835
Diameter of necklace: 4 11/16 in. (11.9 cm)
Height of earrings: 2½ in. (6.4 cm)
Length of belt clasp: 3 9/16 in. (9.1 cm)
Width of brooches: 2 3/16 in. (5.6 cm)
Bequest of Nelson and Juanita Greif Gutman, 1963.
(57.1927-31)

In France in the 1830s and 1840s, machine-stamped jewelry of modest intrinsic value became popular. Characteristic is this parure, or matching suite, that includes a segmented collier, or short necklace, a pair of long pendant earrings, two brooches, and an elongated belt clasp. The pieces are bordered by foliate scrollwork in stamped gold. Each is enameled black and set with half-pearls, emeralds, and diamond sparks in clawed silver collets arranged in rosettes and lozenges. This jewelry is very light in weight and is composed of two layers of stamped metal fastened by pins. Preserved with the jewelry is its case in scarlet, straight-grained morocco leather with symmetrical designs in narrow line gouges and decorative small toolwork, some picked out with colored inlays. Each earring bears a ram's head, the restricted warranty mark for Paris, 1819-38. The necklace bears a tongue marked with an illegible maker's mark in a vertical lozenge.

184

Bracelet

English (?), 1840-50
Length: 8¼ in. (21.0 cm)
Width: 1 9/16 in. (4.0 cm)
Gift of L. Manuel Hendler, 1959. (57.1889)

This bracelet is composed of four oval medallions connected by rings to four concave-shaped interstices. These are enameled in cobalt blue and contain alternating rosette and sprig motifs in gold. Mounted in each medallion in raised flat gold wire are curving tulip plants that radiate from a central emerald in a gold collet. Half-pearls are set in each tulip blossom and leaf. The enameled ovals are bordered by twisted wire. Surrounding the medallions are gold bands of twisted flat wire and alternating spirals and spheres. The enameled interstices are divided by a twisted flat wire. The bracelet closes with a tongue and clasp and is provided with a safety chain.

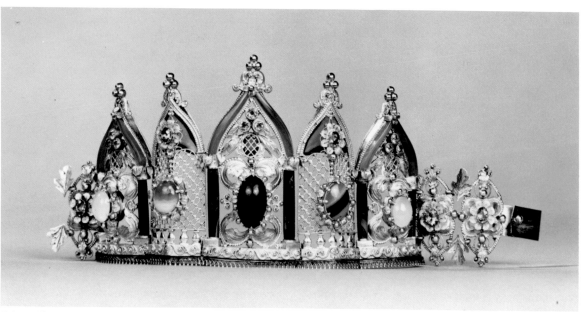

Cat. no. 185

Cat. no. 186 (see colorplate XVIII)

185

Bracelet

Austrian, 1830-70
Length: 7 in. (17.8 cm)
Width: 2¾ in. (7.0 cm)
Publications: Dora Jane Janson, *From Slave to Siren,
The Victorian Woman and Her Jewelry From Neo-
classic to Art Nouveau,* Duke University, Durham,
N.C., 1971, p. 36, no. 64 (ill.).
Collections of anonymous Austrian; Felix Laurence,
Paris; Raphael Esmerian, New York; gift in memory of
Paul Esmerian, 1972. (57.1999)

Five flamboyant gold ogival Gothic arches are hinged
together with the surviving three of five linked foliate
sections to form a bracelet. In the central and largest
arch and in the two end arches, the vaulting, outlined in
carnelian, rises from columns with leafy capitals of gold
and shafts of malachite. Beneath these arches are
cabochon-cut stones—moss agate in the center and
moonstones at the ends—mounted in intricate foliage,
and in their tympana are oval diaper grids backed with
cabochon-cut amethysts and surmounted by three
faceted aquamarines. The two intervening arches are
of gold with tympana of shaped amethysts faced with
gold flowerets set with foil-backed rubies. Below the
tympana are diaper grids in gold, against which are set
cabochon-cut striped agates. All the arches rise from

bases with running scroll and interlocking arcade ornamentation. They are topped by pinnacles with three
spheres surmounting foliate crockets. Two of the three
foliate sections of the bracelet band are mounted with
foil-backed amethysts in gold flowerets, and the other
bears a ruby. Indentations in the fabric liner of the
original leather case indicate that there were once two
other foliate sections.

It has been suggested that this extraordinarily intricate piece of jewelry may have been intended for use
in the theater or at a costume ball. Plausibly, it was
initially a diadem that was later transformed into a
bracelet, with the two missing foliate sections being
used for other purposes, perhaps as earrings.

186

Bracelet

English or Italian, 1860s
Length: 6⅝ in. (16.8 cm)
Width: 1 13/16 in. (4.6 cm)
Gift of Mrs. Bernard Trupp, 1959. (57.1887)

Carved in red coral, the head of Bacchus and the busts
of two bacchantes have been mounted in gold frames
(convex in cross section) festooned with finely chased
blossoms. The flexible band is contrived of cylindrical
gold links chased with floral designs.

Cat. no. 187

Cat. no. 188

187
Brooch with Sulphide Relief

English or American, 1860s
Height: 1⅝ in. (4.1 cm)
Width: 2⅛ in. (5.4 cm)
Gift of Mrs. John N. Adkins, 1972. (57.2014)

A large, oval faceted glass crystal is mounted in an elaborate scrollwork frame of pinchbeck, a copper-zinc substitute for gold. Embedded in the crystal is a white sulphide relief of Leda and the Swan. The sulphide technique of enclosing porcellaneous reliefs within crystals was patented in England by Apsley Pellatt in 1831.

188
Brooch

Swiss, mid-nineteenth century
Height: 1 9/16 in. (4.0 cm)
Width: 1⅞ in. (4.8 cm)
Gift of Mrs. Cyril Keene, 1977. (71.1160)

A stag and a doe are set in a woodland scene minutely carved of horn. The border of overlapping branches is tinted black. Once thought to have originated in Dieppe in the 1840s, such pieces are now believed to have been made in Switzerland for the growing tourist trade in the nineteenth century.

189
Pair of Earrings and Brooch

Venetian (?), 1840s
Height: 2½ in. (6.4 cm)
Collection of Luigi Grassi, Sale, New York, American Art Association, January 1927, no. 414; Mrs. Henry Walters, Sale, New York, April 1941, no. 1278; gift of Melvin Gutman, 1946. (57.1768-69)

The drops of these quartz cat's-eye earrings are surrounded by gold scrollwork set with red, green, and clear stones.

Cat. no. 189

Cat. no. 190

190
Pair of Earrings

Italian (?), 1830s
Height: 2 7/16 in. (6.2 cm)
Acquired before 1931. (44.524-25)

These pieces are characteristic of girandole earrings, a form popularized in the eighteenth century and revived during the 1830s, when women's hairstyles again permitted the display of such jewelry. Wire suspension hooks (now missing) were mounted on the backs of oval silver members faced with painted enamels. These members carry silver openwork floral sections set with variously colored faceted stones from which, in turn, hang the three pear-shaped drops characteristic of the girandole form. In this example the drops are silver faced with painted enamels, rather than the more usual faceted stones. In all the enamels, masked youths and ladies are portrayed. Each earring bears a weevil in a rectangle, the French warranty mark introduced in 1893 for silver imported from countries with customs conventions.

191
Pair of Earrings

French, ca. 1850
Height: 1 in. (2.5 cm)
Acquired before 1931. (44.581-82)

Small earrings became fashionable in France in the 1850s. The heads of this pair in enameled gold are in the form of black-a-moors wearing turbans. Their chests are enameled green. Three small ruby pastes are set in the rims of each of their turbans, and larger oval ruby pastes are mounted in their chests. Each earring bears an eagle's head in double outline without a frame, the Paris restricted warranty mark of gold, introduced in 1847.

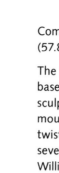

Cat. no. 191

192

Brooch with the Cameo Spring

Italian, after 1874
Height overall: 2 9/16 in. (6.5 cm)
Width overall: 2⅛ in. (5.4 cm)
Height of cameo: 2⅛ in. (5.4 cm)
Publications: Philippe Verdier, "A Rediscovered Cameo After W. H. Rinehart," *BWAG*, vol. 14, no. 8, Baltimore, May 1962, p. 1 (ill.).

Commissioned in Rome by William T. Walters, 1862. (57.854)

The shell cameo showing Spring strewing flowers is based on a lost marble relief executed by the American sculptor William H. Rinehart in Rome in 1874. It is mounted in an Italian gold frame decorated with twisted wire and chain designs. This brooch is one of several known to have been commissioned in Rome by William T. Walters.

193

Pendant

French (possibly Bourg-en-Bresse), nineteenth century
Height: 3⅛ in. (7.9 cm)
Acquired before 1931. (44.520)

A basket of flowers in enameled copper-gilt is suspended by gold chains from an upper gold section. Dangling between the chains is a pink topaz. The chains are composed of double-ringed members strung in the middle with small seed pearls. Both the basket and the top section are enameled pale blue with foliate wheel motifs in pink and white. The flowers are in three tiers: in the lowest tier are small globules of enamel; in the middle, blossoms with individually

Cat. no. 192

Cat. no. 193

enameled petals and stamens; and in the top, three large blossoms in the centers of which are gold bosses set with diamonds. A bird with white and pink plumage is perched in the center of the basket. This attractive, colorful pendant exemplifies the unsophisticated qualities associated with nineteenth-century peasant jewelry. An eagle's head is stamped in a loop on the reverse of the top section.

194

Brooch

French (Normandy), nineteenth century
Height: 3½ in. (8.9 cm)
Width: 2⅞ in. (7.3 cm)
Acquired before 1931. (57.1107)

This brooch is characteristic of peasant jewelry made in areas relatively unaffected by the stylistic developments of the major urban centers. Divided into two segments connected in the center by a looped band, the brooch is rendered in pierced openwork gold and set with small brilliants. The crest at the top of the brooch and several of the sections of the pierced scrollwork are decorated with engraved motifs. This piece has been broken at the upper right side.

The back of the crest bears a maker's mark composed of an illegible letter, a key, and the letter Y in a lozenge; and two warranty marks in the form of an eagle's head (unframed and facing right), similar to the 1838 eagles' heads of Paris. The loop connecting the two members and an adjoining area of the upper member are stamped with a chariot, the restricted warranty mark for the North District of France, 1819-38.

Notes: A more elaborate pendant of this type has been published in M. D. S. Lewis, *Antique Paste Jewellery*, Boston, 1970, pl. 34.

195

Necklace

Italian, before 1903
Length: 14⁷⁄₁₆ in. (36.7 cm)
Believed to have been purchased by Henry Walters from Giacinto Melillo, 1903. (57.1530)

This gold necklace by Giacinto Melillo is in the archaeological style. Alternating opened and closed palmettes are connected by a pair of loop-in-loop chains

Cat. no. 194

extending through eyes on the back of each section. The chains end in clasps of oblongs with palmette terminals bordered in beading. A small frog is mounted on each clasp. All the palmettes are decorated with rosettes, and their petals are delineated by a filigree of tightly twisted wire. Nineteen Egyptian and pseudo-Egyptian steatite and lapis lazuli scarabs in partially beaded frames are attached to the closed palmettes of the spherical beads. On the clasp is the signature *G. Melillo/Napoli.*

Archaeological jewelry refers to nineteenth-century goldsmiths' work simulating in appearance ancient jewelry that had been excavated in Italy. Although there were predecessors, the roman jewelers Fortunato Pio Castellani (1793-1865) and his sons Alessandro (1822-1883) and Augusto (1829-1914) are generally regarded as the principal proponents of the style. Fortunato Pio Castellani was in business in Rome by 1814-15 and by the 1830s had turned to the archaeological style, working in association with the antiquarian Michelangelo Caetani, Duke of Sermoneta (1804-1883).

Cat. nos. 195, 196

Castellani was determined to emulate the marvelous granulation and filigree decoration of Etruscan jewelry, which he had had the opportunity to study at firsthand while advising the Papal government on purchases of goldwork from the Regolini-Galassi tomb discovered at Cervetri in 1836. The eventual partial success of the firm in this endeavor was attributed by the Castellanis to their discovery of peasant jewelers in the village of Sant'Angelo in Vado, where techniques had allegedly been preserved since antiquity. Current research indicates, however, that it was Alessandro Castellani who learned to approximate the ancient technique of applying granulation and filigree with colloidal hard soldering by substituting an arsenite flux with an impalpably

fine solder—a technique he had evolved by the mid-1860s, as was demonstrated at the Exposition Universelle of 1867.

Other notable practitioners of archaeological jewelry included the Neapolitan Carlo Giuliano (1831-1895), who opened a workshop in London in 1860, after having been associated with the Castellanis while they were exiled in Naples following the abortive 1848 revolution in Rome; and Giacinto Melillo (1846-1915), who also trained in Naples with Alessandro Castellani. Giuliano, working in a number of other revivalist styles, became famous for his superb enameling; whereas Melillo apparently adhered to the goldsmith traditions of the Castellanis, although he also turned to silversmithing in the archaeological style, winning the Grand Prix and the Legion of Honor at the Exposition Universelle of 1900.

In April 1903 Henry Walters made substantial purchases at the firm of Giacinto Melillo. Unfortunately, the surviving receipts do not specify the works acquired, many of which were not retained in the Walters' collection. However, it is assumed that this signed necklace and the other unsigned necklace and bracelet (Cat. nos. 196, 197) were acquired on this occasion.

196
Necklace

Italian, before 1903
Length: 14¼ in. (36.2 cm)
Believed to have been purchased by Henry Walters from Giacinto Melillo, 1903. (57.1534)

The beads of this gold necklace in the archaeological style are strung over a concealed loop-in-loop chain. Arranged in sequence are biconical beads, small cylindrical beads from which granulated spherical drops are suspended, and larger cylindrical beads to which intaglios are fastened. The necklace ends in eye loops, which may have been connected by an S-hook (now missing). The cylindrical beads are decorated with tightly twisted wire loops. Engraved on the Roman intaglios, which are variously colored in sardonyx, moss agate, striped agate, and rock crystal, are representations of ancient deities and heroes. Each intaglio is mounted in a gold frame decorated with twisted wire with gold bosses at each side and triangles of ten granules each at the bottom. The piece is attributed to Giacinto Melillo.

197
Bracelet

Italian, before 1903
Length: 7½ in. (19.1 cm)
Believed to have been purchased by Henry Walters from Giacinto Melillo, 1903. (57.1532)

This gold bracelet in the archaeological style consists of a band of twelve Roman intaglios variously colored in chalcedony, sardonyx, and moss agate. The intaglios are separated by bars composed of three rods con-nected by wire loops and mounted on a pair of loop-in-loop chains. At the top and bottom of the frame of each intaglio is a triangle of granules. The bracelet is fastened by two pairs of pin-and-socket connectors. The piece is attributed to Giacinto Melillo.

198
Ring

French, mid-nineteenth century
Diameter: ¾ in. (1.9 cm)
Height of bezel: ½ in. (1.3 cm)
Collection of Henry Walters; Laura F. Delano; gift of Laura F. Delano, 1946-47. (57.1779)

This neo-Renaissance gold ring has a raised hexagonal fluted bezel with a miniature portrait of a lady in sixteenth-century costume under cut diamond. The convex hoop, enameled and set with diamonds, has winged terminal figures at the shoulders. The ring bears an unframed eagle's head, the Paris restricted warranty mark for gold, 1838-47.

Cat. no. 197

Cat. no. 198

Cat. no. 199

199

Brooch

Italian, early nineteenth century
Diameter: 2 in. (5.1 cm)
Collection of George W. Kosmak, M.D.; gift of Miss
Katharine Kosmak and Mr. George Kosmak, October
1975. (43.46)

Executed in fine-glass tesserae, this circular mosaic
shows the waterfalls at Tivoli. The plain gold frame is
equipped with a pin and eye.

Notes: Glass tesserae mosaics produced in the Vatican workshops
figured prominently in the Papal States' displays in nineteenth-
century expositions and were a common item in the tourist trade.

200

Brooch

Italian, mid-nineteenth century
Height overall: 2¹/₁₆ in. (5.2 cm)
Width overall: 1½ in. (3.8 cm)
Height of medallion: 1⅞ in. (4.8 cm)
Gift of Mrs. J. Griswold Webb, March 1979. (41.257)

Mounted in a gold frame is an oval grey-lava medallion
with the head of a pseudo-classical bacchante carved in
high relief. The frame is decorated with a single strand
of twisted wire. Lava jewelry generally originated in the
region of Pompeii. This example is preserved in a black
leather case bearing within its lid the name and address
TIFFANY & CO. / [550] B.WAY / NEW YORK. Tiffany &
Co. was located at 550 Broadway from 1854 until 1870.

Cat. no. 200

201

Horse-Head Stickpin

American or English, ca. 1880
Diameter of pinhead: ⅞ in. (2.2 cm)
Length: 3⅛ in. (7.9 cm)
Presumed to have been purchased by William or Henry
Walters at Tiffany & Co. (57.1122)

The horse's head on this gold pin is carved in intaglio in
the crystal and then naturalistically painted. The pin
bears the name TIFFANY/CO.

Notes: Reverse painted intaglios of animals were made popular in
England in the 1860s by the firm of Hancock and Co. The technique
was subsequently adopted by Tiffany & Co., New York (see Charlotte
Gere, *American and European Jewelry,* New York, 1975, p. 195).
There is some question as to whether such stickpins with intaglios
were manufactured in the United States or imported from England by
Tiffany & Co.

202

Tiepin with Tooth

American, 1875-1900
Length of pin: 3 in. (7.6 cm)
Length of tooth: ³¹/₃₂ in. (2.5 cm)
Acquired before 1931. (57.1238)

An incisor is mounted by a gold chain to the bead head
of this gold pin. The shaft of the pin is twisted.

203

Black-a-moor Stickpin

French, mid-nineteenth century
Length: 3¾ in. (9.5 cm)
Acquired before 1931. (44.583)

The head of this gold pin is in the form of a black-a-
moor with an enameled face. Both his turban and chest

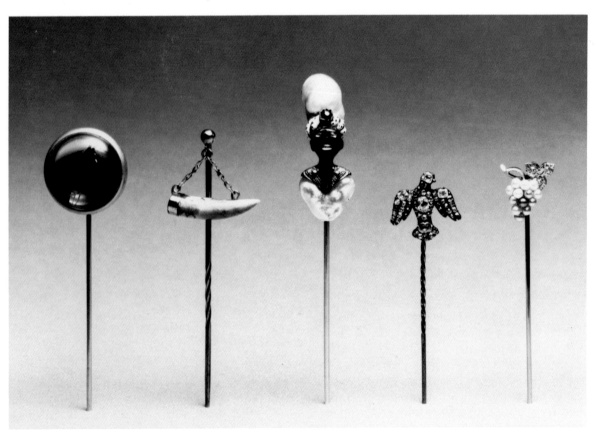

Cat. nos. 201, 202, 203, 204, 205

are baroque pearls. The rim of the turban is in white enamel with diagonal rows of black dots and is set with a red paste. This decorative motif was introduced to France from Italy in the eighteenth century. The pin bears an unframed eagle's head in double outline, the Paris restricted warranty mark introduced in 1847, and an illegible anvil mark.

204

Eagle Tiepin

American, 1875-1900
Length: 2 $7/16$ in. (6.2 cm)
Width of eagle: ¾ in. (1.9 cm)
Acquired before 1931. (57.1109)

The head of this pin is in the form of an eagle rendered in pavé-set small diamonds. It is hinged to the gold pin, which is twisted to grip the fabric of the tie.

205

Stickpin with Grapes

American, ca. 1910
Length: 2⅞ in. (7.3 cm)
Bequest of August Mencken, 1967. (57.1984)

The head of this pin is in the form of a cluster of grapes made of thirteen seed pearls of varying hues. Three leaves are added, each of gold faced with platinum inset with a small brilliant.

Notes: The pin belonged to the donor's brother, H. L. Mencken. It is preserved in its original, unmarked leather case.

206

Iris Corsage Ornament

American (New York), ca. 1900
Height overall: 9½ in. (24.1 cm)
Height of blossom: 2¾ in. (7.0 cm)
Publications: Anonymous, *Tiffany and Co.'s Exhibit, Paris Exposition Universelle,* New York, 1900, p. 5.
Believed to have been purchased by Henry Walters at Tiffany & Co. (57.939)

Made by Tiffany & Co., this fabulous large brooch is in the form of an iris naturalistically treated. Set with

faceted blue sapphires varying in intensity of color and hue as well as in size, the blossom is comprised of three standards, or upright petals, and three falls, or drooping sepals, in oxidized silver, beneath which are three small-style branches in etched gold. The 120 sapphires in the brooch are all listed in the Tiffany & Co. catalogue as being of American origin. Ribs of diamond sparks set in platinum have been applied to the three falls and to two of the standards. The bearding of the falls is suggested by citrines mounted in shaped gold collets. The blossom emerges from a long, etched gold stem, from which spring three leaflets, or spathes, rendered in demantoid garnets mounted à *jour* in gold frames. The ornament bears the monogram TCO.

The famed firm of Tiffany & Co. began in New York in 1837 as the fancy goods shop Tiffany and Young; four years later it became Tiffany, Young and Ellis. Included in the early stock were goods imported from the Orient and fine-quality paste jewelry. In 1848 the Paris branch opened, and in 1853 two partners withdrew from the business, leaving Charles Lewis Tiffany (1812-1902) sole proprietor until 1868, when the firm was incorporated. Under the direction of Edward C. Moore, Tiffany's Silver Department won international acclaim for its innovations, among them the importation of Japanese techniques and designs; however, Tiffany & Co. was best known in the late nineteenth century for its spectacular jewelry characterized by the lavish use of precious stones. Tiffany's success in this regard can in part be attributed to its gem specialist, George F. Kunz, the distinguished mineralogist and champion of American gems and pearls.

207

Pearl Pendant

American (New York), 1900-1910
Length of chain: 20 in. (50.8 cm)
Weight of pearl: .2 oz. (4.7 g)
Purchased by Henry Walters from George F. Kunz at Tiffany & Co., New York; he subsequently presented it to his niece Laura Delano; gift of Miss Laura F. Delano. (57.2034)

Mounted in a platinum cage is one of the largest pink pearls in existence—an ovoid mauvish pink pearl of the Common Conch (Strombus gigas). The cage, which is

Cat. no. 206

Cat. no. 207 (see colorplate XIX)

hinged at the base to open, is comprised of five bands of leaves and blossoms rendered in platinum set with minute diamond sparks. Surmounting the cage is a foliate cluster, which turns to allow the bars to be disengaged. The pendant is suspended from a long trace chain of equal oval links. Every thirtieth link is set with a diamond spark. The pendant bears an eagle's head, the mark of restricted warranty.

208
Nautical Ring

American (New York), 1893
Diameter: $^{19}/_{32}$ in. (1.5 cm)
Length of stone: $^7/_8$ in. (2.2 cm)
Acquired before 1931. (57.1123)

A large aquamarine, with its table engraved to show a bell and a compass, is set in a gold ring. The shoulders are in the form of mermaids holding anchors. Their tails intertwine to complete the shank. Large fish accompany the mermaids. This ring presumably belonged to Henry Walters, who was an enthusiastic yachtsman. The ring bears a globe superimposed on the letter T, the mark applied to wares made specially for the World's Columbian Exposition, Chicago, held in 1893. The ring has been kept with its original chameleon-skin box marked *Tiffany & Co./New York/Paris-London.*

Cat. no. 209 (see colorplate XX)

209
Lalique Pendant and Necklace

French, ca. 1902
Length of chain: 22 in. (55.9 cm)
Height of pendant: 3⅛ in. (7.9 cm)
Publications: Henri Vever, *La bijouterie française au XIXe siècle,* III, Paris, 1906-1908, p. 739 (ill.); Barten, *René Lalique,* p. 330, no. 678; Emile Sedeyn, "A travers les Expositions," *L'Art Decoratif,* vol. 14, Paris, 1903, p. 229.
Acquired by Henry Walters at the Saint Louis World's Fair, 1904, as *No. 53, Pendant.* (57.941)

This partially draped piece features a female figure holding a pitcher ("La Source"). Carved of bone, the figure is surrounded by wisteria vines, the stalks of which are enameled deep blue; the leaves, green; and the blossoms, opalescent white. Rounded pale orange Mexican opals are set in the vines above the figure's head on either side and below her feet. The chain is composed of elongated blue enameled links and gold (?) rings. The reverse of the pendant is carefully

Cat. no. 208

tooled but not enameled. The name *LALIQUE* is marked on the left edge.

René Jules Lalique, who was born in Ay in 1860 and died in Paris in 1945, was one of the most imaginative designers in the history of jewelry. He utilized a wide array of precious and non-precious materials to create works that bridged the traditional division between the fine and the industrial arts. After training in Paris and briefly in London, Lalique began to draw designs for the leading jewelry houses in Paris, producing a number of compositions for naturalistic floral pieces rendered in diamonds. In 1885 he was able to acquire the fully manned and equipped atelier of Jules d'Estape and to turn to the fabrication of his own pieces. Five years later he established a larger studio with fittings of his own design on 20 rue Thérèse. It was here, between

1891 and 1895, that two series of jewels were produced for the actress Sarah Bernhardt in her roles of Iseyl and Gismonda. In 1895, the year he received a third-class medal for a controversial figurative corsage at the exhibition of the *Société des Artistes français,* his jewelry was also featured among the works in various media assembled by Samuel Bing for the *Salon de l'Art nouveau,* which represented the most progressive international artists of the period. Perhaps the apogee of Lalique's career as a jeweler was the *Exposition universelle* of 1900. Many of the extraordinary, large, and at times bizarre pieces produced for this event have been preserved in the Calouste Gulbenkian Foundation in Lisbon. Although he continued to exhibit jewelry in international exhibitions at the beginning of this century, Lalique's interests were gradually being diverted

Cat. no. 210 (see colorplate XXI)

to the manufacture of art glass. In 1909, the year he received a contract from Coty for the production of perfume bottles, Lalique acquired a glass works at Combes-la-Ville near Paris, and in 1921 he moved to a larger factory at Wingen-sur-Moder, Alsace, where until World War II he continued to produce the molded glass for which he is noted.

It was at the Saint Louis World's Fair of 1904 that Henry Walters purchased the Lalique jewelry presently in the collection. The Walters' pieces are not among those listed in the French Section of the *Catalogue général officiel de l'exposition universelle de Saint-Louis* (Paris, 1904, p. 44), and therefore they were presumably shown in Lalique's own exhibits of *Objets et bijoux d'art,* no. 27, in Département D, Manufactures, Palais des Manufactures.

210
Lalique Opal and Diamond Brooch

French, ca. 1903-1904
Height: 2¾ in. (7.0 cm)
Width: 5 7/16 in. (13.8 cm)
Publications: Barten, *René Lalique,* p. 414, no. 1060A.
Acquired by Henry Walters at the Saint Louis World's Fair, 1904, as *No. 34, Pin.* (57.935)

A large cushion-shaped opal is mounted in a silver-gilt frame set with small diamonds of varying size. Extending laterally are diamond-set stalks that terminate in two layers of fern leaves. Mounted with prongs, the four uppermost leaves are of opalescent cameo glass tinted with soft hues of green and silver enamel. The lateral segments are hinged to the central unit to permit movement. The name *LALIQUE* is marked at the top edge of the opal mounting.

211
Lalique Brooch with Fruit Clusters

French, ca. 1903
Height: 1 7/16 in. (3.7 cm)
Width: 2½ in. (6.4 cm)
Publications: Barten, *René Lalique,* p. 412, no. 1053.
Acquired by Henry Walters at the Saint Louis World's Fair, 1904, as *No. 24, Pendant... one pink pearl 38½ g. 1/32.* (57.942)

A large pale pink pearl is surrounded by leaves and fruit of laurel extending from a short central stalk. The branches are enameled brown, and the leaves are covered with thin white translucent enamel. The clusters of fruit are carved of opals. The name *LALIQUE* is marked on the reverse of the top right leaf.

212
Lalique Brooch with Nude Woman

French, ca. 1902
Height: 1½ in. (3.8 cm)
Width: 2¾ in. (7.0 cm)
Publications: Barten, *René Lalique,* p. 321, no. 650.1.

Cat. no. 211

Cat. no. 212 (see colorplate XXII)

Cat. no. 213 (see colorplate XXIII)

Acquired by Henry Walters at the Saint Louis World's Fair, 1904, as *No. 22, Pendant.* (57.944)

This brooch is in the form of a kneeling nude woman — her body turned at the waist and her arms raised behind her head — placed against a curvilinear, symmetrical gold framework set with small diamonds. Enameled, auburn-colored hair cascades behind her. The name *LALIQUE* is marked in the center of the bottom edge.

213

Lalique Tiger Necklace

French, ca. 1903-1904
Diameter of necklace: 4½ in. (11.4 cm)
Length of teeth: 2⅜ in. (6.0 cm)
Width of reliefs: 2⅛ in. (5.4 cm)

Publications: Randall, "Jewellery Through the Ages," p. 79, fig. 19; Institute for the Arts, Rice University, and The Art Institute of Chicago, *Art Nouveau, Belgium, France,* 1976, no. 415; Barten, *René Lalique,* p. 247, no. 349.
Purchased by Henry Walters at the Saint Louis World's Fair, 1904; listed separately in surviving invoices. (57.938)

Reliefs of horn carved with striding cats alternate with pointed, brown tortoise shell shaped as feline incisors. Beneath each cat is a polished, rounded triangle of brown agate mounted in gold. A claw extends from each side of the relief. The teeth and claws are set in gold mounts that are hinged together to form the necklace. The greenish gold sections are worked to suggest foliage and are tinted with brown enamel. The name *LALIQUE* is marked on the clasp.

Glossary

Aglet. An ornament designed to be sewn to a garment.

A jour. An open style of setting that exposes all the facets of a stone.

Almandine. A deep red or purplish type of garnet.

Baroque pearl. A large irregularly shaped pearl often used by Renaissance goldsmiths to form the head or torso of an imaginary creature.

Beaded wire. Wire with a grooved pattern pressed into it.

Beveled. The plane formed by two surfaces at some angle less than a right angle.

Bezel. The top part of a ring, containing the stone, device, or other ornament.

Bloodstone, or heliotrope. A type of chalcedony composed of plasma with dots of red jasper. Used frequently for seal stones.

Boss. A raised ornamentation, similar to a knob, that protrudes from an object.

Botonée. Decorated with rounded or trefoil ends.

Box setting. A setting in which the stone is secured by a rectangular metal frame.

Brilliant cut. A style of cutting a stone into fifty-eight facets. Used mostly for diamonds.

Cabochon. A style of polishing that gives a stone a smooth, rounded top surface.

Carnelian. A translucent and usually dull red quartz that has a waxy luster.

Cast. To form an object by pouring a metal in a liquid state into a mold, thus making an impression of that mold when the metal hardens.

Chalcedony. A type of milky quartz that is bluish grey, greenish, or yellowish, the varieties of which are agate, carnelian, and chrysopase.

Champlevé. Enamel that is fused over a field of metal where the colors merge and blend.

Chasing. The ornamentation of sheet metal by indenting from the front with a hammer, chisels, and punches.

Citrine. A type of quartz that ranges in color from pale yellow to a reddish hue.

Cloison. An enclosure made of strip metal that surrounds enamel or a cut stone.

Cloisonné. Enamel divided by partitions of metal secured to a base of metal.

Demantoid garnet. A green type of garnet.

Electrum. An alloy of silver and gold known as ''white gold.''

Email en résille sur verre. A process in which a design is cut into a piece of glass or rock crystal. The depressions are lined with a thin piece of gold foil, which is then filled with translucent enamels.

Email en ronde bosse. An enameling process in which the enamel is adhered to figures modeled in high relief. Often used on the ornate pendants so popular during the Renaissance period.

En cabochon. Cut in the cabochon style.

Engraving. The process of cutting away a surface (metal or other) with a sharp instrument in order to create a linear design.

Faience. A general term for glazed earthenware.

Fibula. A brooch resembling a safety pin used in early times to secure folds of clothing.

Filigree. A type of ornament in which thin strands of gold or silver wire are twisted and soldered into patterns.

Finial. A crowning ornament or detail.

Flange. A band set inside a bezel that holds the stone firmly in place.

Foil. A thin sheet of metal put under a paste or gemstone to enhance its brilliance or color.

Granulation. A technique of soldering tiny metal balls onto a metal surface.

Grisaille. A type of enamel painted with dark and light colors of similar hue to give a monochromatic effect.

Haematite. A blue-black opaque stone often used for intaglio seal stones and beads.

Hoop. The part of a ring that surrounds the finger.

Hyacinth, or **jacinth.** This name refers to both an orange-red garnet and to a zircon of similar color.

Inlaying. The process of setting a decorative material (usually a precious stone or piece of colored glass) into the surface of another substance, usually metal, without elevating the surface of the ground material.

Intaglio. An engraving or incised design cut below the surface of a stone or piece of metal. When the stone or metal is pressed into a softer substance, an image in relief is made.

Jasper. An opaque quartz that varies widely in color (brown, yellow, red, green) due to its large number of impurities, most frequently iron.

Jet. Black lignite that takes on a brilliant sheen when polished.

Lapis lazuli. An opaque dark blue silicate with white dots.

Malachite. A translucent or opaque green stone mottled with dark or light bands.

Matrix. A section of the parent rock in which a mineral is embedded.

Meerschaum. A fine, clay-like substance, whitish in color, that becomes hardened and totally white when heated.

Nicolo. A type of onyx frequently used for cameos or intaglios.

Niello. Any of several metallic alloys of sulfur with silver, copper, or lead that give a deep black color. Used for decorating silver and, less frequently, gold.

Opal. A semi-transparent, milky white stone with shimmering rainbow-like effects.

Parure. A matching set of jewelry that usually consists of a necklace, brooch, bracelet, and earrings.

Pavé setting. A setting in which small stones secured by metal prongs are arranged in close proximity to one another.

Pectoral. A decorative piece worn on the breast that is either pinned like a brooch or hung as a pendant.

Pendeloque cut. A style in which a stone is first cut in the shape of a tear and then faceted with a brilliant cut.

Penannular. Almost circular in shape.

Plasma. A dark green type of chalcedony similar to jasper in composition.

Plique à jour. Enamel used over an openwork design so that the light strikes it from the back.

Repoussé. The working of sheet metal in relief by using a hammer and punches on the reverse side.

Rock crystal. A colorless, transparent quartz, differentiated from glass by its properties of greater hardness, coldness, and double refraction.

Rose cut. A cut with twenty-four facets that resembles an unopened rosebud in shape.

Sard. A translucent brownish red chalcedony often used for seals.

Sardonyx. A type of chalcedony that has parallel red and white stripes, the red being sard.

Shoulders. The sections of a ring hoop closest to the bezel or central ornament.

Steatite, or **soapstone.** A brown or greyish green type of talc.

Strapwork. A type of ornamentation in which flattish metal bands or strips are interwined into decorative patterns.

Table cut. A style of cutting that gives a stone a flat, table-shaped surface. A table-cut stone is often surrounded by a beveled edge or smaller facets.

Tourmaline. A greenish blue or light blue stone used as a gem.

Verre eglomisé. An intricate method of painting on glass that is first coated with gold leaf. The outline of the design is traced onto the gold leaf, then covered, and the remaining gold leaf removed. The outline is painted in, and finally the piece is varnished and backed with a reflecting metal foil. The technique reached its peak during the Renaissance.

Abbreviations

ABC
Antiquités du Bosphore Cimmerien.
Imperial Archaeological Commission,
St. Petersburg, 1854.

Aldred, *Jewels*
Aldred, Cyril. *Jewels of the Pharaohs:
Egyptian Jewelry of the Dynastic
Period.* Praeger, New York, 1971.

Alexander, *Jewelry*
Alexander, Christine. *Jewelry: The Art
of the Goldsmith in Classical Times.*
The Metropolitan Museum of Art, New
York, 1928.

Barten, *René Lalique*
Barten, Sigrid. *René Lalique: Schmuck
und objets d'art, 1890-1910.* Munich,
1978.

Becatti, *Oreficerie*
Becatti, Giovanni. *Oreficerie antiche,
dalle minoiche alle barbariche.* Rome,
1955.

Breglia, *Napoli*
Breglia, Laura. *Le oreficerie del Museo
Nazionale de Napoli.* Rome, 1941.

BMCJ
Marshall, Frederick H. *Catalogue of the
Jewelry, Greek, Etruscan, and Roman,
in the Departments of Antiquities,
British Museum.* London, 1911.

Byzantine Art
The Walters Art Gallery. *Early Christian
and Byzantine Art.* Baltimore, 1947.

Canby, *Ancient Near East*
Canby, Jeanny Vorys. *The Ancient
Near East in The Walters Art Gallery.*
Baltimore, 1974.

CMS
*Corpus der Minoischen und Myken-
ischen Siegel.* Akademie der wissen-
schaften und der literatur, Mainz.
Berlin, 1964.

The Dark Ages
Worcester Art Museum. *The Dark
Ages.* Worcester, Massachusetts,
February 20-March 21, 1937.

Deér, "Mittelaltarliche Frauenkronen"
Deér, Josef. "Mittelaltarliche Frauenkronen in Ost und West," *Monumenta
Germaniae Historica,* Schriften, vol.
13/2. Stuttgart, 1738-1951.

"Exhibition of Gold," *BCMA*
"Exhibition of Gold," *The Bulletin of
the Cleveland Museum of Art,* no. 9.
November 1947.

Furtwängler, *AG*
Furtwängler, Adolf. *Die antiken Gem-
men, Geschichte der Steinschneide-
kunst im Klassischen Altertum.* 3 vols.
Leipzig-Berlin, 1900.

Greifenhagen, *Berlin I*
Greifenhagen, Adolf. *Schmuck-
arbeiten in Edalmetall.* Staatliche
Museen Preusischer Kulturbesitz,
Antikenabteilung. Berlin, 1970.

Greifenhagen, *Berlin II*
Greifenhagen, Adolf. *Schmuck-
arbeiten in Edalmetall.* Staatliche
Museen Preusischer Kulturbesitz,
Antikenabteilung. Berlin, 1975.

Hackens, *Classical Jewelry*
Hackens, Tony. *Classical Jewelry.*
Museum of Art, Rhode Island School
of Design, Providence, 1976.

Hadaczek, *Ohrschmuck*
Hadaczek, Karl. *Der Ohrschmuck der
Griechen und Etrusker.* Vienna, 1903.

Higgins, *Greek and Roman Jewellery*
Higgins, Reynold A. *Greek and Roman
Jewellery.* London, 1961.

Hoffmann and Davidson, *Greek Gold*
Hoffmann, Herbert and Patricia F.
Davidson. *Greek Gold: Jewelry from
the Age of Alexander.* Mainz, 1965.

The Marlborough Gems
Story-Maskelyne, M. H. Nevil. *The
Marlborough Gems.* Vol. 1, London,
1780; vol. 2, London, 1791, illustrated
by Bartolozzi; reissued, London, 1845.

Muller, *Jewels in Spain*
Muller, Priscilla E. *Jewels in Spain,
1500-1800.* The Hispanic Society of
America, New York, 1972.

Otchët
*Otchët Imperialistichago Archeolog-
icheskago Obshchestva.* Saint Petersburg, irregularly from 1888.

Pareti, *Regolini-Galassi*
Pareti, Luigi. *La tomba Regolini-Galassi.* Rome, 1947.

Petrie, *Amulets*
Petrie, W. M. Flinders. *Amulets, Illustrated by the Egyptian Collection in The University College, London.* London, 1914.

Pfeiler, *Römischer Goldschmuck*
Pfeiler, Barbara. *Römischer Goldschmuck des ersten und zweiten Jahrhunderts n. Chr. nach datierten Funden.* Mainz, 1970.

Randall, "Jewellery Through the Ages"
Randall, Richard H., Jr. "Jewellery Through the Ages." *Apollo.* December 1966.

Randall-MacIver, *Villanovans*
Randall-MacIver, David. *Villanovans and Early Etruscans.* Oxford, 1924.

Romans and Barbarians
Museum of Fine Arts. *Romans and Barbarians.* Boston, 1977.

Ross, *Migration Period*
Ross, Marvin C. *Arts of the Migration Period.* Baltimore, 1961.

Ross and Downey, "An Emperor's Gift"
Ross, Marvin C. and Glanville Downey. "An Emperor's Gift—And Notes on Byzantine Silver Jewelry of the Middle Period." JWAG, vols. 19-20, 1956-57.

Steindorff, *Catalogue*
Steindorff, George. *Catalogue of the Egyptian Sculpture in The Walters Art Gallery.* Baltimore, 1946.

Steingräber, *Alter Schmuck*
Erich Steingräber. *Alter Schmuck.* Munich, 1956.

Strøm, *Etruscan Orientalizing Style*
Strøm, Ingrid. *Problems Concerning the Origin and Early Development of the Etruscan Orientalizing Style.* Odense, 1971.

Zahn, *Galerie Bachstitz*
Zahn, Robert. *Galerie Bachstitz, s'Gravenhage, II, Antike, byzantinische, islamische Arbeiten der Kleinkunst und des Kunstgewerbes, Antike skulpturen.* Berlin, 1921.

Zahn, *Schiller*
Zahn, Robert. *Sammlung Baurat Schiller, Berlin, Werke antiker Kleinkunst.* Auction-Catalogue. Rudolph Lepke's Auctions-Haus, Berlin, March 19-20, 1929.

Periodicals

AA
Jahrbuch des Deutschen Archäologischen Instituts. Archäologischer Anzaigen

AJA
American Journal of Archaeology, (from 1885)

AK
Antike Kunst, (Olten, from 1958)

BCH
Bulletin de Correspondance Hellenique, (Paris, from 1877)

BMMA
Bulletin of The Metropolitan Museum of Art, (New York, from 1905)

BWAG
Bulletin of The Walters Art Gallery, (Baltimore, from 1948)

CIL
Corpus Inscriptionum Latinarum, (Berlin, from 1882)

Drevnosti
Drevnosti Trudy Imperatorskago Moskovskago Archeologicheskago Obshchestva

JIAN
Journal International d'archéologie numismatique, (Athens, from 1898-1927)

JRGZM
Jahrbuch des Römisch-Germanischen Zentralmuseums Mainz, (Mainz, from 1954)

JWAG
Journal of The Walters Art Gallery, (Baltimore, from 1938)

NSc
Notizie degli Scavi di Antichità, (Rome, from 1876)